We would like to thank the following artists and illustrators: Howard Pyle, N. C. Wyeth, Frank Schoonover, George Varian, George Albert Williams, Louis Rhead, Stephen Read, Richard Rodgers, Charles Dixon and Harris & Sons. Most of the images are from books in the editor's collection. Two images are courtesy of Dover Publications - Blackbeard, page 25, and the Flying Dutchman inside the back cover. The text for the 50 individual pirates is from the Allen & Ginter cards published in 1888. Additonal text by Jay Humphreys. Cover design by Shaun Aunchman. The photographs are from Treasures by Marc Anthony in St. Augustine, Florida.

Index to the 50 Pirates of the Spanish Main:

HANDBOOK OF 50
PIRATES

SHIPS, WEAPONS, FLAGS, MAPS, TREASURE & STORIES

Handbook of 50 PIRATES

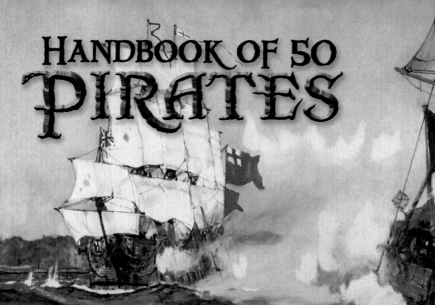

©2008 Historic Print & Map Company Printed in the USA
www.handbookofpirates.com ISBN 978-0-9729463-6-0
Designed, compiled and edited by Henry Hird III

Pirates, Buccaneers, and Privateers

PIRATES! Throughout the centuries, there are few words that can match this one for its ability to create feelings of adventure, dread or even spine-chilling fear. For countless generations, pirates have been a topic sparking the imaginations of young and old alike. From Treasure Island to today's big screen depictions of pirate life, the story of piracy on the open sea never grows old. Unfortunately, these popular descriptions of pirate life and lore seldom match the realities of life as a seagoing bandit — a hard, and often cruel existence that held the promise of wealth untold, but more often than not delivered misery and an untimely death.

Despite the prospects of death at sea or at the end of a hangman's rope, there were thousands of men (and women) who avidly pursued "the sweet trade" — as piracy was sometimes described. Whether disenchanted with the often unrewarding and backbreaking work as a sailor in the service of a king, discouraged by the economic returns of honest labor, or just desperate for adventure, pirates sought out a career on the high seas. All pirates sought out the riches aboard treasure-laden ships or carried by rich merchantmen, but there were differences between these treasure-hunters.

Preying on the treasure-laden Spanish galleons sailing home from the Spanish Main, the buccaneers terrorized the Caribbean. Their name came from the French backwoodsmen who lived on the island of Hispaniola and smoked meat by using a boucan (barbecue). For those who wanted to be a pirate, but were a little reluctant to become total outcasts from society, there was always the possibility of becoming a privateer — a pirate with a letter of marque signed by a king or government official that gave permission to rob and plunder ships from an enemy country. Pirates were known by many names, including filibuster and freebooter. But no matter what they were called, the exploits of the pirates were truly the stuff of legend.

Ships used by Pirates

THE SLOOP was the most popular pirate ship. It had everything a pirate needed — it was fast so it could chase down merchant ships — and outrun pursuers. Its small size allowed it to hide in coves that were too shallow for warships to enter. But it could carry a large pirate crew, the booty they captured and enough cannons to stop their victims. Pirate schooners were larger and faster than sloops, but like the brigantine, they could not easily hide. Often seen in movies, large three-masted frigates with numerous cannons were used only by a few very successful pirates.

FRIGATE had three masts with square rigged sails and was the largest and most powerful type of ship used by pirates.

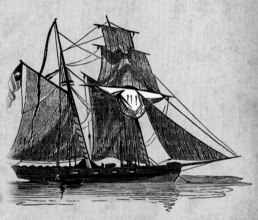

SCHOONER had two masts with fore-and-aft rigged sails and was the fastest type of ship used by pirates.

BRIGANTINE had two masts with square rigged sails on the foremast and fore-and-aft sails on the main mast. It was a versatile ship that was reasonably fast and had a large cargo capacity.

SLOOP had one mast with fore-and-aft rigged sails and was the smallest and most common type of ship used by pirates.

A SPANISH GALLEON was heavily armed and carried the riches of the New World home to Spain. The large ornately decorated galleon was the dream target of pirates.

5

4

Prese
and I

Admirals Flag

T

Crows

R

Front View of the Ship

Sea
Compass

Stern

Crew lifting the Anchor off the bottom

Keel of the Ship

KETCH

Back — Front

Mizzenmast

5. 10. 15. 20. 25

Mainma

Stern

Profile of a Ketch

Capstan

Hold

Rudder

6

...tion of a WARSHIP *with complete Rope, Sailwork, Flags*
...ners. Also showing Bow and Stern views.

Side View of the Bow

Ratlines

NORTH

WEST

EAST

SOUTH

Bow

Stern View

Buoy or Anchor Watchers

Cross Staff

Fore
Mast

Bowsprit

Guns

Bow

Profile of Boat

7

FLAGS OF PIRATES

N.C. Wyeth · Treasure Island

EDWARD ENGLAND

STEDE BONNET

JACK AVERY

FLAGS are among the most recognized symbols of piracy. The famous "skull and crossbones" is thought of as the standard flag of a pirate, but in reality buccaneer banners came in many designs and colors. The term "Jolly Roger" was derived from the French "Jolie Rouge" meaning "pretty red" — the red flag that by law had to be flown by English privateers. Black became the color of choice for the flags of the most famous pirates. In fact, some pirates went to great effort to be associated with their personal flags in hopes that their quarry would simply surrender when they recognized the flag of their pursuer.

JACK RACKAM

BART ROBERTS

THOMAS TEW

EDWARD TEACH

CHRISTOPHER MOODY

CAPTAIN WORLEY

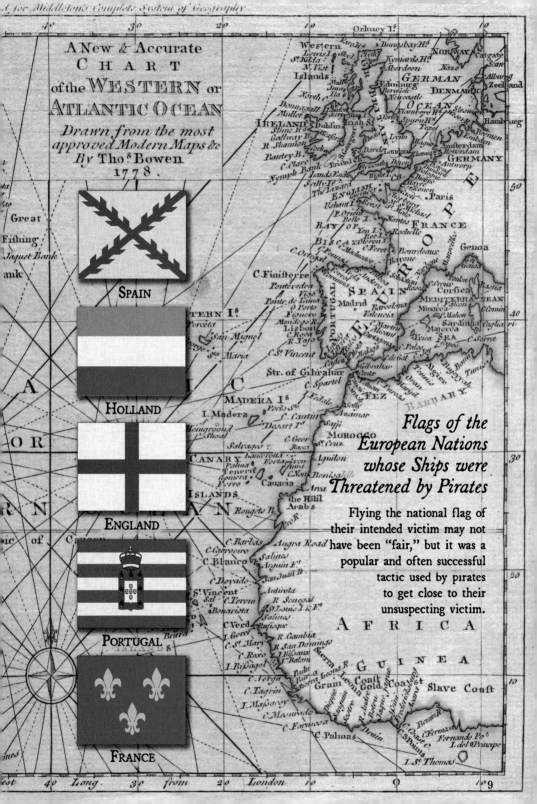

Flags of the European Nations whose Ships were Threatened by Pirates

Flying the national flag of their intended victim may not have been "fair," but it was a popular and often successful tactic used by pirates to get close to their unsuspecting victim.

WEAPONS OF PIRATES

WHEN SELECTING WEAPONS, pirates needed two types — cannons that could stop or slow a ship and small arms that would allow them to quickly overpower their opponents in hand-to-hand combat. As they approached their victim, pirates fired cannons to "knock" down her masts and rigging while other pirates picked off crewmembers with muskets. Because pirates only needed to disable their prey, they preferred relatively small cannons that were light enough to accomplish their goal without slowing their ship's speed with excess weight. Getting nearer, pirates swept the decks of their opponent with blasts from swivel guns that were like small cannons mounted on the ship's railing. Pulling alongside, the pirates used grappling hooks on ropes to lash their ship to their victim. Then, armed with a variety of bladed

weapons, the pirates would swarm aboard the entrapped merchant ship. Boarding pikes were thrown like spears, while boarding axes were used to chop through locked hatches and anyone who resisted their onslaught. The cutlass, a short sword with a slightly curved blade, was the most popular weapon among pirates — it was perfect for fighting in a crowd. Pirates also stabbed their victims with daggers or threw short knives known as dirks. The pirate blunderbuss was a short, heavy musket that could spray small iron balls, nails or scrap metal — a single shot could easily kill several people. A flintlock pistol was useful in a fight, but reloading it took time that wasn't available in the heat of battle. As a result, some pirates carried several loaded pistols. Of course, clubs, fists and even teeth were used in these desperate fights. No matter what weapons they carried, the fight for control of a ship was always hand-to-hand, brutal and bloody.

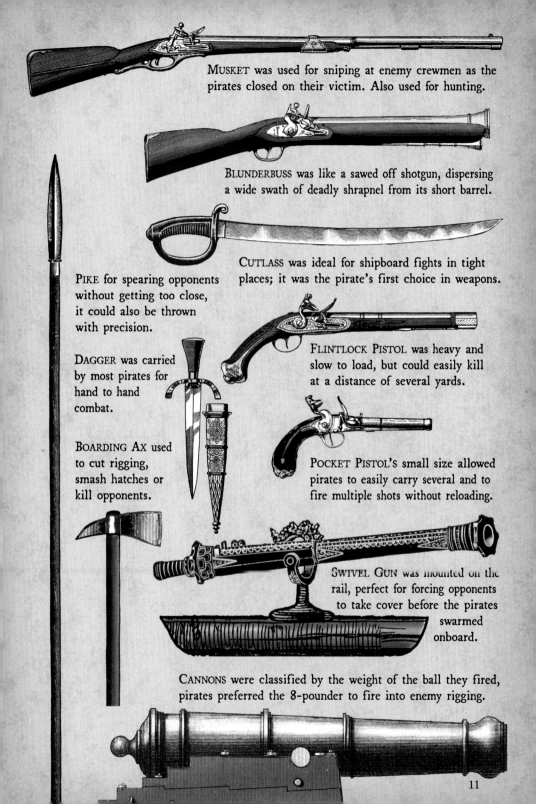

MUSKET was used for sniping at enemy crewmen as the pirates closed on their victim. Also used for hunting.

BLUNDERBUSS was like a sawed off shotgun, dispersing a wide swath of deadly shrapnel from its short barrel.

CUTLASS was ideal for shipboard fights in tight places; it was the pirate's first choice in weapons.

PIKE for spearing opponents without getting too close, it could also be thrown with precision.

DAGGER was carried by most pirates for hand to hand combat.

FLINTLOCK PISTOL was heavy and slow to load, but could easily kill at a distance of several yards.

BOARDING AX used to cut rigging, smash hatches or kill opponents.

POCKET PISTOL'S small size allowed pirates to easily carry several and to fire multiple shots without reloading.

SWIVEL GUN was mounted on the rail, perfect for forcing opponents to take cover before the pirates swarmed onboard.

CANNONS were classified by the weight of the ball they fired, pirates preferred the 8-pounder to fire into enemy rigging.

Articles of Conduct

Pirates were outlaws, but they were anything but lawless. Each crewmember of a pirate ship followed a "code" that was often agreed upon before sailing, that allowed them to be treated fairly and honestly — far more fairly than did the laws imposed by kings on their subjects. These were some of Barthlomew Robert's articles of conduct.

1. Every man has a vote in affairs of moment: has equal title to the fresh provisions or strong liquors at any time seized, and use them at pleasure unless a scarcity makes it necessary for the good of all, to vote a retrenchment.

2. If they defrauded the Company to the value of a dollar, in plate, jewels or money, marooning was the punishment.

3. No person to game at cards or dice for money.

4. The lights and candles to be put out at eight o'clock at night. If any of the crew after that hour still remained inclined to drinking, they were to do it on open deck.

5. To keep their piece, pistols and cutlass clean and fit for service.

6. No boy or woman to be allowed among them. If any man was found seducing any of the latter sex, and carried her to sea disguised, he was to suffer Death.

7. To desert the ship or their quarters in battle, was punished by Death or Marooning.

8. No striking another on board, but every man's quarrels to be ended on shore, at sword and pistol.

9. No man to talk of breaking up their way of living till each had a share of £1,000. If, in order to do this, any man should lose a limb or become a cripple in their service, he was to have 800 dollars out of the public stock, and for lesser hurts proportionably.

10. The Captain and Quarter Master to receive two shares of a Prize; the Master, Boatswain & Gunner, one share and a half and other Officers, one and a quarter.

11. The musicians to have rest on the Sabbath day, but the other six days and nights, none without special favour.

PUNISHMENT

PIRATES LIVED IN A CRUEL WORLD where torture and painful punishment were commonplace. Captives were sometimes tortured in an attempt to get information about the location of hidden treasures. Pirates who broke "the code" were often punished for their misdeeds by their fellow pirates.

KEEL-HAULING

Captured pirates knew they were likely to receive a death sentence carried out by hanging — an event they referred to as "dancing the hempen jig." Despite their reputation for cruelty, most pirates merely inflicted the same punishments that were commonly used in the Royal Navy of that time. Beatings with a whip-like cat-o'-nine tails could result in permanent injury while keel-hauling — towing a bound victim from one side of a ship to the other by pulling them beneath the ship's hull could result in death. Some small chance for survival was offered to those who were marooned — abandoned with only a jug of water and a pistol on a small island that would probably be underwater at high tide. Despite the popular notion of walking the plank, there is little evidence that such a punishment was used. It was much easier to simply toss the unfortunate soul overboard.

Maps and Navigation in Dangerous Waters

THE ABILITY TO FIND the trade routes sailed by the wealthy merchant ships and then to find the way home with looted treasure was essential for successful pirates. Without a good navigator, pirates

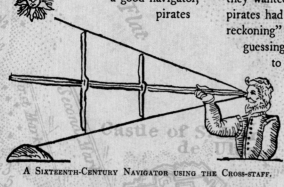

had to simply hope they would end up at their desired destination. By using these valuable tools, the navigator could tell his pirate shipmates not only where they were, but how to get where they wanted to go. Without them, pirates had to rely on "dead-reckoning" which was basically guessing, or sailing close to shore to sight landmarks in order to find their way.

A SIXTEENTH-CENTURY NAVIGATOR USING THE CROSS-STAFF.

Cross-staff: Used to find latitude by measuring the sun's altitude at midday.

SPYGLASS: Also known as a telescope or the "bring-'em-near," to identify ships from long distances or to sight important landmarks.

ASTROLABE: Used to determine latitude, day or night, by taking sightings of the sun or specific stars.

OCTANT: Invented in 1733, it improved the navigator's ability to determine latitude by sighting the sun or stars even when the ship was rolling in heavy seas.

NOCTURNAL: Employed at sea for finding the hour of the night by the North Star.

COMPASS: Simple and efficient, the compass needle always points North.

NOCTURNAL: Used to tell time after sunset and before sunrise.

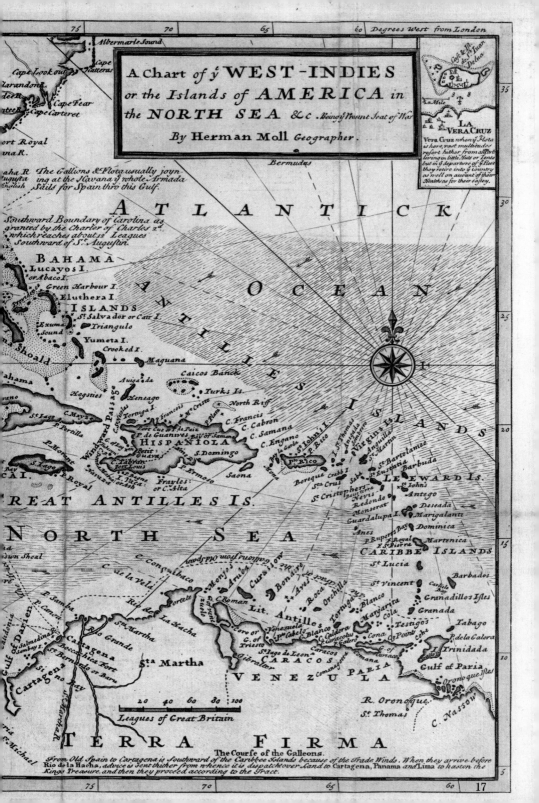

Albemarle Sound

Cape Look out   Cape Hatteras

Clarandon   Cape Fear
deete   Cape Carteret

ort Royal
na R.

A Chart of ỹ WEST-INDIES or the Islands of AMERICA in the NORTH SEA &c. Being ỹ Present Seat of War
By Herman Moll Geographer.

Cast le. S. Juan de Ulua

LA VERA CRUZ

La Mile

Vera Cruz when y Flota is here, vast multitudes resort hither from all Parts living in little Huts or Tents but on y departure of y Fleet they retire into y country as well on account of their Healthas for their Safety.

aha R.
uguta
English

The Gallions & Flota usually joyning at the Havana y whole Armada Sails for Spain thro this Gulf.

A T L A N T I C K

Bermudas

Southward Boundary of Carolina as granted by the Charter of Charles 2d which reaches about 12 Leagues Southward of St Augustin.

BAHAMA
Lucayos I.
or Abaco I.

Green Harbour I.

Eluthera I.

ISLANDS
St Salvador or Catt I.

Exuma
Sound   Triangulo

Yumeta I.
Crooked I.

O C E A N

G R E A T   A N T I L L E S   I S.

 na Shoal

ahama

Hogsties

St Iago C. Mays I.
P. Pertilla

P. Morent

St Iago
B. Royal

CAI.

Maguana

Auigada

Heneago

Caicos Banck

Turks Is.

North Riff

C. Cristo   Palos
Fort Cue   B. de la Paix
P. de Guanves
Petit Guave
Tiburon
Port Louis
J. Vaca
L. Vache orashe
Manuel orash

C. Francis
C. Cabron
C. Samana

St John I.

HISPANIOLA

S. Domingo

Frayles
or C. Alta

Saona

C. Engano

Pla de Sama
P. Rico

Boruke Crabb I.

Sta Cruz

Bill of Samana

P. Ermoso

St Thomas
Virgins
Anagada
Anguilla
St Martin

Le Rico

St Bartolamee
Saba
St Eustatia

LE EWARD Is.

St John's

ANTILLES   ISLANDS

N O R T H   S E A

id
own Shoal

C. Consalvaco

C. de la Vela

Rio de la Hacha

P. Samba
P. Canoa
St Salmedina
Samby I.
Cartagena
Boca chica Fort
St Bernardo or Baru
Cartagen
no Bay

Portete

St Martha

Lowds P10 from Gronessa

Monjes

Aruba

C. Roman

St Martha

Rio Grande

Coro
G. of
Triesto
St Pedro Cabello
Venezuela
Caldera
St Iago de Leon
Gibralter
CARACOS
VENEZUELA

Lit. Antilles

Bondry

Aves Island

Boca

Blanco
Caldera
Caracobu
Calera

Orchilla

Tortuga
Blanco

Cona

Margarita
Cola

G. of
Comango

P. Royal
F. Pierra

Anes

R. Rupert's Bay

Guardalupa I.

Redondo
Monserat
Nevis
St Christophers

St Lucia

St Vincent

Grenadillos Isles

Testigos

G. of Curacoa

G. of Paria
PARIA

Antego
Deseada
Marigalanti
Dominica
Martenica

CARIBBE   ISLANDS

Barbados

Carlisle Bay

Granada

Tabago
P. de la Galera

Trinidada

Gulf of Paria

Orono que Isles

R. Oronoque.
St Thomas

C. Nassou

20   40   60   80   100
Leagues of Great Britain

T E R R A   F I R M A

The Course of the Galleons.
From Old Spain to Cartagena is Southward of the Caribbee Islands because of the Trade Winds. When they arrive before Rio de la Hacha, advice is Sent thither from whence it is dispatchover Land to Cartagena, Panama and Lima to hasten the Kings Treasure, and then they proceed according to the Tract.

PIRATE TREASURE

THE THIRST FOR TREASURE was the motivation that drove most pirates to a life of seagoing lawlessness. Pirates dreamed of capturing a Spanish galleon loaded with tons of gold and silver — most had to be satisfied with less lucrative booty. Even so, one pirated gold doubloon was worth more than what an honest seaman would earn in nearly two months.

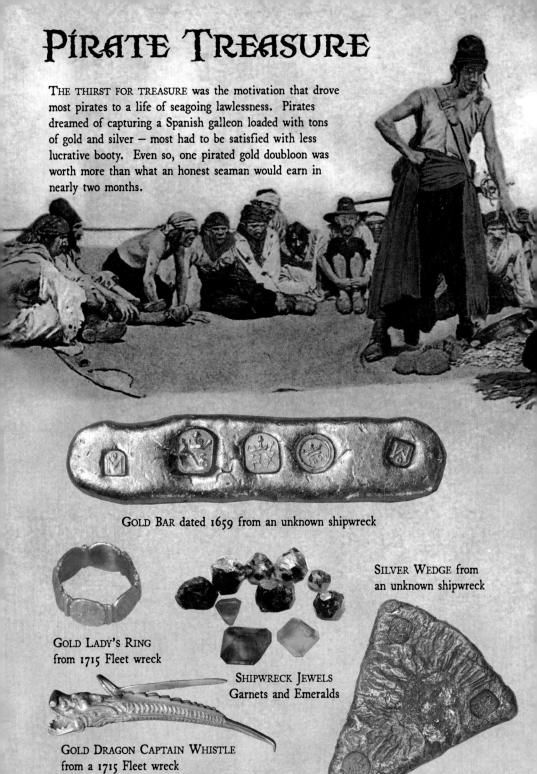

GOLD BAR dated 1659 from an unknown shipwreck

GOLD LADY'S RING from 1715 Fleet wreck

SHIPWRECK JEWELS Garnets and Emeralds

SILVER WEDGE from an unknown shipwreck

GOLD DRAGON CAPTAIN WHISTLE from a 1715 Fleet wreck

GOLD 4 ESCUDO
King Phillip V
Spanish dated 1711
from a 1715 Fleet wreck

GOLD 8 ESCUDO *front and back*
King Phillip IV Seville Mint
from early 1600s

GOLD BUST DOLLAR
8 Escudo Carlos IV
Spanish dated 1799

SILVER COB
Spanish Phillip V
from a 1715 Fleet

GOLD & EMERALD
CROSS AND CHAIN
from a 1715 Fleet wreck

SILVER PILLAR DOLLAR
minted in Mexico
dated 1739

19

ALLEN & GINTER *Manufacturers of*
PIRATES of the SPANISH MAIN

PIRATES OF THE SPANISH MAIN is the name of the set of 50 tobacco cards published by Allen & Ginter in 1888. Each card was 1-1/2" x 2-3/4" and inserted into a pack of cigarettes. The front featured the face of a pirate with an action scene in the background. Each card also had a narrative text on the back. Allen & Ginter marketed the first cigarette cards for collecting and trading, a marketing gimmick to encourage people to buy more cigarettes.

This *Handbook of Pirates* includes all 50 pirate cards including the complete text about each pirate.

Index to the 50 PIRATES OF THE SPANISH MAIN:

Captain Kidd

There are but few persons in the United States who have not heard the name of the renowned pirate, Captain Kidd. There are, also, but few to be found who have any intelligent conception of his wild and infamous career. In the year 1695, William III, of England, became alarmed at the daring exploits of the desperate pirates who infested the American coast and the West Indies, and threatened to destroy all commerce. The King determined to fit out an expedition against them; and, while seeking for a commander, he was informed that just the man he wanted had recently arrived in London from New York. He was no other than William Kidd, then a successful merchant, a man of tried courage and integrity. Armed with the royal commission, Captain Kidd set sail from Plymouth, England, in 1696. We may suppose, however, that even at this time he had a suspicion that he might wish to steal a ship and turn pirate himself. This in reality happened. Having cruised about for a long time without sighting a single pirate, his men became desperate. The state of Kidd's own mind may be judged from the fact that when a large Mongol ship, richly freighted, hove in sight, although an ally of England, he bore down upon her, and seized her as his prize. He was now guilty of an overt act, and from this time alas for the ship that was so unfortunate as to meet him! Meanwhile the British Government had officially proclaimed him a pirate, and he was finally captured at Boston in 1699. Thence he was taken to England, tried for piracy and murder, and hanged at Execution Dock, London, May 12, 1701.

English Coat of Arms

Above is the letter of marque, a privateering commission from King William III of England. It gave permission for William Kidd to legally attack anyone who threatened English commerce. Below is Captain Kidd and crew burying treasure on Gardiners Island near New York.

Above is an attack by Captain Kidd on one of his crew, killing him. Below is Captain Kidd after he was tried and hanged in England.

EDWARD TEACH, BLACKBEARD

EDWARD TEACH, (BLACK BEARD).

Walking the Plank.

NEXT TO THE NAME of Captain Kidd, the most famous, perhaps, of all piratical names is that of Captain Edward Teach or "Blackbeard," as he was called. He was a real, ranting, raging pirate, who buried pots of treasure, and made many a luckless prisoner walk the fatal plank. Teach was a Bristol man, and learned his trade on board sundry privateers in the West Indies-an admirable school. About the year 1716 he was made captain of one of the prizes. Blackbeard's fortune was made. The distinction between "privateer" and "pirate" was only that of a few letters, and Mr. Blackbeard found it an easy step to make the change. For a time he plied

BLACKBEARD'S FLAG

his trade down on the Spanish Main. Then he took a notion to try his luck on the Carolina coast. So off he sails with his little fleet, and blockades the port of Charleston, capturing incoming and outgoing vessels at his pleasure. Having obtained about $8,000 from these prizes, he sailed away to North Carolina, and surrendered himself to the Governor, taking advantage of the King's pardon which had recently been proclaimed. Nevertheless he held tight to his ill-gotten wealth. Soon he was off again flying the black flag. But this time the bold Capt. Blackbeard did not fare so well; for the traders and planters, wearied beyond endurance with such an unmitigated pest, besought the Governor of Virginia for aid. Accordingly Lieutenant Maynard was dispatched to Ocracoke Inlet to fight this pirate. A battle of the utmost desperation ensued. Blackbeard fought like a tiger. At length he fell, pierced by twenty-five wounds, and the surviving pirates were only reserved that they might be hanged. Surely, "the way of the transgressor is hard."

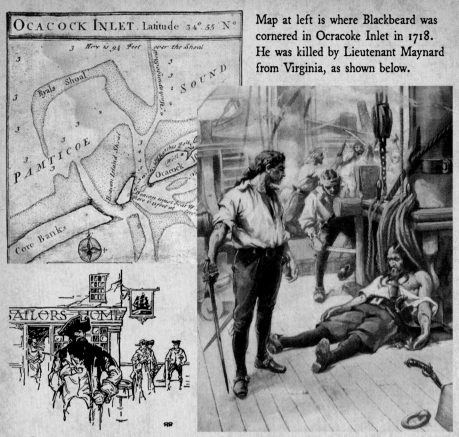

Map at left is where Blackbeard was cornered in Ocracoke Inlet in 1718. He was killed by Lieutenant Maynard from Virginia, as shown below.

CAPTAIN AVERY began his extraordinary career as mate of a stout English ship, the "Duke." While in the West Indies he became impressed with the advantages offered by piracy as an easy and lucrative means of livelihood. He was a man of more cunning than courage. He despised the captain, and determined to run away with the ship. So, wasting no time, he formed a conspiracy among the desperate men on board, quietly raised anchor at night, turned the captain adrift, and sailed for Madagascar. Upon the Arabian coast he fell in with a great ship, sailing under the Mogul's colors. He ran her down, clapped her on board, and took the ship by storm. The vessel proved to belong to the Great Mogul himself. His own daughter was on board, bound on a holy pilgrimage to Mecca, with the richest treasures to present at the shrine of Mohammed. The booty obtained from this prize was immense. Having concluded that he had earned enough money by his trade, he determined to retire from the business, and live in ease the rest of his days. So he set about to secure the best of the booty for himself, and then directed his course to Boston, Massachusetts; but not liking the looks of the town, he crossed to Ireland, and proceeded to dispose of his jewels. He put them in the hands of a Bristol merchant, who undertook to act as his broker, and that was the last the pirate ever saw of his Indian treasures. Utterly beggared, he was stricken with a fever and died, and was buried at the expense of the parish as a vagabond pauper.

JACK AVERY was known to have used both a red and a black flag.

JACK AVERY.

Capturing ship of the Great Mogul.

Sir Henry Morgan

The limits of this sketch will afford the barest outline of the eventful career of Sir Henry Morgan, for no pirate before nor since his time ever conducted operations on so grand a scale. He was associated with Mansvelt in the conquest of St. Catherine's Island, and a little later began his independent depredations upon Spanish towns by taking Puerto Principe, a rich inland city of Cuba. He made off with a vast deal of plunder; and, as soon as it had been divided, commenced active preparations to sack Porto Bello, and that city's doom was sealed. Next to suffer were Maracaybo and Gibraltar, now just recovering from the desolations lately wrought by Francis Lolonois. Then this very able, though infamous, leader laid his plans for a new expedition which was to eclipse all that was ever done before. By the middle of December, 1670, his squadron of 37 vessels, manned by 2200 veteran pirates, was in readiness. So, choosing a certain Bradley for vice-admiral,

Morgan sailed away from Hispaniola, intent upon taking the great city of Panama. On the way he captured the stronghold of St. Catherine and Chagres. Then, leaving his ships, he began the weary march across the Isthmus of Panama, situated on the western or Pacific Coast. The city fell after a desperate conflict and now followed the usual sequence of events-rapine, cruelty and extortion. At length the pirates departed with their immense treasure. At the division, Morgan, a consummate knave, adroitly managed to secure most of it for himself; and then retired from business, honored by all, knighted by the king, and rewarded with the post of Governor of fair Jamaica.

SIR HENRY MORGAN.

Thomas Anstis

IN THE YEAR 1718 Howel Davis, Walter Kennedy, and Thomas Anstis seized the "Buck" sloop belonging to Governor Woods Rogers, of New Providence, and ran off a-pirating. Not long afterwards, Bartholomew Roberts joined their number. Then was organized what we may call the "Big Four" combination of piratical days, which afterwards became so formidable. Thomas Anstis for some time commanded a brigantine, which served as a tender to Roberts; but, as this position was not commensurate with the greatness of his soul, he determined to bid Roberts a "soft farewell," as he called it. Accordingly, one dark night in the month of April 1721, he changed his course, and steered for the West Indies. The following June he captured a number of vessels. Their crews were ofttimes treated in the most barbarous manner. Just in the midst of this prosperous cruise a mutiny sprang up among his own crew, and the majority were in favor of mending their ways, and petitioning the king for pardon. A petition was dispatched, and the pirates while awaiting the issue withdrew to an uninhabited island near Cuba, a secluded retreat. Here they spent about nine months amid the usual debaucheries of a pirate's rendezvous. At length Anstis received word that his pirates' petition was not favorably regarded in England. "We'll turn no hairs gray for that," he said. So he ordered his men on board, and immediately resumed his piratic career. At length a party of malcontents put an end to his career by shooting him dead while asleep in his hammock.

THOMAS ANSTIS.

The Pirates Retreat.

Michael le Basque

MICHAEL LE BASQUE.

Each man with a Prisoner.

THERE WAS AT TORTUGA a notorious sea-robber by the name of Michael le Basque. In his younger days he had seen wide service with the French army in Europe. Later he came to America, turned freebooter, and acquired great wealth by cruising. With only forty men he surprised Maracaybo by night, locked up the principal inhabitants in the cathedral, and then fell to pillaging everything that was portable. Daylight disclosing his feeble force, he was forced to retreat; but each man drove before him a prisoner which he held for ransom. Not long afterwards this same

buccaneer cut out a large treasure ship, the "Margaret," from under the very guns of Portobello, and made off with her together with a million dollars in coined money which she contained. Having now grown rich and famous, he settled down at the buccaneer retreat at Tortuga, and was appointed major of the island. Thus he remained in retirement until at length his piratic zeal was fired anew by the proclamations of the indomitable Lolonois. He proposed to this pirate to become a partner in his enterprises, and his assistance was only too gladly accepted. With eight ships and a crew of five hundred picked desperadoes they swooped down upon the city of Maracaybo like the blast of a plague. The city of Gibraltar, lying forty leagues to the southward, was the next to suffer; and when at length the pirates spread their sails, they left behind an awful scene of smoldering ruins and bare desolation. It is probable that Le Basque returned with the victorious fleet to Tortuga, but his after history is lost in the mists of the past.

SAMUEL BELLAMY

SAMUEL BELLAMY.

Wreck of the Whydaw

SAMUEL BELLAMY became a declared enemy to mankind about the year 1717. His first capture was a staunch ship bound from Jamaica to London, with a rich cargo of ivory and gold-dust. The prize not only enriched, but also strengthened him. He immediately mounted her with 28 guns, and collecting a crew of one hundred and fifty men, as desperate as himself, he shaped his course for Virginia. Such was the beginning of the cruise of the dreaded pirate ship Whidaw, which later wrought such mischief on the New England coast. For a time Bellamy and his jolly company cruised about the Virginia Capes, and were rapidly squeezing that region dry when they were driven out to sea by a terrific hurricane, and it was with the greatest difficulty that they kept that ship afloat. After many days the weather cleared up, and they arrived off the coast of Rhode Island in safety. Here they passed the time very jovially. Among their diversions was the acting of a play called "The Royal Pirate," which was written by a certain waggish fellow of their number, and was performed on the quarter-deck amid great applause. Finally, as the warm days advanced, they concluded to pass the summer on the Maine coast, and so departed, picking up a sloop on the way, from which Captain Bellamy took on board, for his further satisfaction and enjoyment, a choice stock of wines. In the autumn our jolly crew steered southward again, and were having things very much to their liking, when, one night, during a drunken revel, they ran ashore on the bleak Cape Cod coast, and not one of them escaped to tell the tale.

WRECK OF THE PIRATE SHIP WHIDAH.

33

BARTHELEMY

ONE OF THE BOLDEST and most renowned buccaneers, was a Portuguese, named Barthelemy. Roused by rumors of adventures which promised gold and glory, he followed the tide of emigration to the West Indies. At Kingston, Jamaica, he fitted out a small sloop in which to prey upon Spanish commerce. He had been

out but a few days, when he captured a great ship, with a cargo valued at a hundred thousand dollars. Barthelemy did not long enjoy his ill-gotten spoil, however, for a few days later, he was overpowered by three large Spanish ships, and taken to Campeche for execution. But the wily Portuguese was not thus to be outdone. At dead of night, he contrived to escape to the shore. He took to the woods, and

began a painful struggle through the entanglements of a tropical forest, barefoot, bleeding, starving, tracked by blood-hounds and pursued by bands of Spaniards. At length he reached a large open bay; procured a boat and thirty men; and breathing revenge, steered for Campeche. Gliding into the harbor at midnight, he surprised the vessel from which he had so recently escaped, closed the hatches upon the sleeping crew below, and exultingly steered for the sea. Barthelemy, as he sailed away under a cloudless sky, boasted loudly of still greater enterprises he would undertake. Lost in his ambitious imaginings he did not notice a small cloud which appeared in the horizon. Rapidly it increased, and a tropical tornado burst upon the ship. She went to pieces on the rocks like a cockle-shell, and Barthelemy and a few of his companions found themselves utterly beggared upon a lonely isle. What eventually became of him we know not, but we are told that "he was never successful after."

PORTUGUESE BARTHELEMY.

The wreck

MAJOR STEDE BONNET

THERE WAS IN BARBADOES a gentleman of wealth, position and education, by the name of Major Stede Bonnet. He fitted out, entirely at his own expense, a sloop with ten guns and seventy men, with the avowed purpose of preying upon Spanish commerce. But, weighing anchor at night, he steered for the Capes of Virginia, and immediately fell to plundering all vessels he encountered, disposing of their crews in the usual piratical fashion. At length he met, in rogue's company, another piratic ship, commanded by one Capt. Teach, who, from the mass of intensely black hair which covered his face, was commonly called Blackbeard. Finding that the Major knew little about maritime affairs, Blackbeard determined to relieve him of the "cares and fatigues of commanding a vessel," as he termed it. So he seized the Major, took him on board his own ship, and added the "Revenge" to his piratic squadron. Just before Blackbeard surrendered to the king's proclamation, Bonnet got command of the "Revenge" once more, and likewise availed himself of His Majesty's pardon. But like Teach, he soon found his way back to his evil courses, and jogged along snugly enough till the brave Colonel Rhet caught him in Cape Fear River. A considerable quantity of powder and ball was required to bring down the black flag of the pirates. But then the gallant colonel had the honor of bringing into Charleston as pretty a lot of villains and cutthroats as the town ever saw. One month later they were all strung up in a row at White Point, near the provincial city of Charleston.

STEDE BONNET'S FLAG

STEDE BONNET.

Surrender of Bonnet

ANNE BONNY

ANNE BONNY.

Firing upon the crew

AMONG THE REMARKABLE RECORDS of piratical days appear the strange though well-accredited careers of two female pirates, Anne Bonny and Mary Read. The history of the latter is given in another sketch. Anne Bonny was born near Cork, but while yet a child was taken by her father to Carolina. Here the girl grew up in the possession of a fierce and ungovernable temper. However her prospects were considered good for a desirable marriage, as she was heir to a good fortune; but she spoiled all by eloping with a worthless sailor who took her to the Island of Providence. Here she met Captain Rackam the pirate, who persuaded her to marry him and run away to sea disguised as his cabin boy. It so happened that Mary Read was on board the same ship; and, in the many bloody engagements which followed, none were more courageous than these two young sailor women. When the English frigate took the pirate, as is told in the life of Captain Rackam, every one fled from the storm of grape-shot into the hold except Mary Read and Anne Bonny. Mary, it was said, called to those under decks to come up and fight like men. As they refused, she fired her pistol down among them, killing one and wounding others; but such bravado was not at all in accordance with her general character. It was, however, just the conduct to be expected of Anne Bonny. At the trial, they were both found guilty of piracy, and condemned to be hanged; but Anne Bonny was reprieved from time to time, and finally escaped execution. What at length became of her we do not know.

Samuel Bradish

BRADISH

Depositing his jewels

In the days of Captain Kidd, the seas were swarming with pirates. Among these desperadoes was a pirate by the name of Bradish, whose career in the popular mind became blended with that of Kidd. Bradish sailed from England, in 1697, on a voyage to Borneo, as boatswain of a ship which, by a strange coincidence, bore the same name as that in which Kidd sailed from New York a few years before — the "Adventure." At the island of Polonais the vessel stopped for water, and the Captain and several of the officers went ashore. Bradish, a desperate fellow, conspired with several of the sailors; seized the ship; silently spread the sails; and stood out to sea.

The wide world lay before him. The boundless ocean spread the wealth of its commerce for his plunder. Among the cargo there were about $40,000 in coined money. This sum Bradish shared among his piratic crew. He then cleared the decks, and directed his course for America. We have no account of the vessels captured on the way. Upon reaching Long Island, he went ashore, and carried with him money and jewels amounting to a large sum, and deposited them with a confederate there. He then ran along the coast to Block Island. Here the company separated into two portions, each party taking its share of the remaining treasure. Many of the pirates landed on the Connecticut shore, and dispersed throughout the country. They behaved very civilly, and paid abundantly for all they bought. At length the rumor of their landing spread; the country was alarmed; and Bradish and about eighteen of his men were arrested, sent to England, tried, and duly executed.

Captain Bradley

BRADLEY

The taking of Castle Lawrence

ACCOMPANYING SIR HENRY MORGAN'S great expedition against the opulent but unfortunate city of Panama, was a certain Captain Bradley. This fiercely brave desperado was made vice-admiral of the piratic squadron; but before the fleet could sail it was necessary that wide regions should be devastated and several towns sacked, merely to obtain provisions for the army. Accordingly, Bradley was dispatched with four ships upon a foraging expedition to the South American coast. He plundered and tortured the poor Spaniards, mercilessly. Then, with ships heavily freighted with provisions, he returned

to the piratic rendezvous. The united fleet, consisting of thirty-seven sail and 2200 pirates, now swept down upon the island of St. Catherine. Next to fall was Chagres, a strongly fortified settlement on the Atlantic shores of the isthmus. Captain Bradley led the expedition. Three days' sail brought his fleet to its destination. High on a precipitous crag commanding the entrance to the harbor, stood Castle Lawrence, bristling on all sides with cannon. The buccaneers hesitated before attempting the assault of works so formidable; but after much perplexity it was resolved to make the attempt. Like a host of demons they rushed up the ascent. Hundreds fell, and Bradley himself had one leg carried away, but he refused to leave the field until he saw the pirates' blood-red flag planted upon the castle walls. Morgan soon joined his victorious advance guard, and pursued his march to Panama. Amidst the succeeding scenes Bradley's name is lost, and we hear of him no more.

Capt. Howel Davis

HOWEL DAVIS.

Taking a Dutch Treasure Ship.

THE NAME OF CAPTAIN HOWEL DAVIS stands high among his fellow pirates. The African coast was his favorite cruising ground and stratagem his favorite weapon. While he was still plying his trade down on the Spanish Main, he hoodwinked the captain of a French man-of-war; and, by a sudden show of force, intimidated him into the surrender of his craft without the firing of a single shot. In a similar manner, he surprised and overpowered the Governor and guards of Gambia Castle, Africa; locked them all up in the guard room, and then sailed away with a good snug sum to share amongst his desperate companions. As they cruised down the coast, they spied a sail, and immediately gave chase. The vessel, a Dutch treasure ship, endeavored to run ashore; but Davis perceiving the design, gave her a broadside whereupon she immediately struck. The prize proved to be exceedingly rich, containing more than a hundred thousand dollars in coin. Their courage growing high with success, they determined to take the island of Del Principe. Davis laid his plans carefully and well, and would have succeeded, only a Portuguese negro among his crew, swam ashore in the night and disclosed the plot to the Governor of the fort. Accordingly the next day when Captain Davis came ashore, he and his companions were received with great civility and were immediately conducted toward the Governor's mansion. But on the way a careful ambush had been laid; and at a given signal there was a sudden volley of musketry, a cloud of smoke, and when the cloud lifted, there lay Captain Davis and all his men stretched dead upon the ground.

Alexander Bras de Fer

About the time that Lolonois, in command of a powerful fleet, was engaged in his fiendish exploits, there was a singular adventurer at Tortuga by the name of Alexandre Bras-de-Fer, who, in his small way, was engaged in making history with as earnest a purpose as his illustrious contemporary. This brave and prudent sea-robber never joined in large expeditions, preferring to sally forth in his swift cruiser, with no one to share or subtract from his gains. On one occasion when Alexandre was bound upon an expedition of great consequence, he was overtaken by a scorching tropical calm, which was followed some days later by a furious tornado. The pirate crew were suddenly stranded upon a lonely isle. Not many days after, a large ship approached, attracted by the pure water which the island afforded. Presently a boat was lowered, and a well armed party of Spaniards cautiously landed. Bras-de-Fer laid a careful ambush; and at a given signal, the buccaneers rushed fiercely upon the Spaniards, and slew them to a man. Then they donned the dress of their victims; and thus disguised, pulled out to the ship. Not until they had clambered up the sides were they recognized. The surprise was sudden and complete. In a few minutes the rich ship was a prize to the buccaneers, and Alexandre triumphantly sailed away to seek other adventures.

ALEXANDER BRAS-DE-FER.

In ambush.

Captain Condent

CAPTAIN CONDENT.

Shooting the Indian.

CAPTAIN CONDENT was a Plymouth man born, and turned pirate without leaving any especial reasons for the step. When Governor Rogers scattered the pirates from New Providence, Condent took occasion to withdraw in a sloop belonging to a certain Mr. Simpson, a Jew merchant of New York. He directed his course for Cape Verde Islands. On the way, it is said, he had a mortal encounter with an Indian who had collected most of the arms into the hold, and threatened to blow up the ship. The danger was imminent; there was no time for parley. Condent leaped into the hold. The Indian instantly fired. A moment later Condent fired, and the Indian fell dead at his feet. In due time the pirates reached Cape Verde Islands, and plundered the entire salt fleet, consisting of twenty sail. Sailing down the coast, Condent exchanged his sloop, in piratic fashion, for a fine Dutch frigate. Then he crossed to Brazil, where he plundered many rich merchantmen, and maimed and tortured their crews in a most barbarous manner. Afterwards he again directed his course across the Atlantic, rounded the Cape of Good Hope, and steered for the East Indies. The plunder gathered in during this cruise was immense. As he returned he took a great ship of seventy guns, richly laden with plate and money. The pirates brought her into a secluded harbor, and shared the vast treasure. They then retired, each with an ample fortune, to the island of Mascarenhas, where they received the royal pardon, and disbanded their company.

CAPTAIN CONDENT'S FLAG

John Davis

JOHN DAVIS.

Stabbing the Sentry.

THE BOLD JOHN DAVIS, native of Jamaica, was one of the earliest adventurers who conducted invasions by land. For some time he had cruised about Jamaica and Carthagena, and not a single sail appeared in sight. At length, rendered desperate by ill fortune, he resolved to invade Nicaragua, and sack the town of Granada.

With only eighty men he swooped down upon the great city in the darkness of the night, silenced the sentinel with the thrust of a sword, and then fell to pillaging dwellings, warehouses, and churches alike. They quietly entered the houses of the chief citizens, seized the inmates, and compelled them on pain of death, to surrender all their jewels and money. They then broke into the churches, gouged out the jeweled eyes of images, and hammered up the altar plate into convenient lumps of metal. Of course, it was but a short time before the whole city was in an uproar. The alarm bells began to ring and the citizens to rally in the market-place, and there was nothing left for Davis and his handful of pirates but to retreat to the boats. Nevertheless they carried with them coined money and jewels to the value of fifty thousand pieces of eight as well as a number of the wealthy Spaniards, whom they held for ransom. They had scarcely regained their boats when a band of five hundred horsemen dashed down to the waterside, but too late to intercept their retreat; and the pirates triumphantly spread their sails and slowly disappeared.

EDWARD ENGLAND

NED ENGLAND was a pirate of a different sort from many of those whose lives we have had occasion to chronicle. He was a rollicking, good natured fellow who would have been perfectly contented with a moderate amount of plunder, and less villainous deeds; but he was often overruled by his wicked associates. Ned began life as mate of a Jamaica sloop; was taken by pirates; and, not long after, himself appeared as master of a piratical sloop. Chased from the Spanish main by English men-of-war, he steered for Africa, and, during the summer of 1719, succeeded in making those hot regions still hotter for the dozen or more merchantmen that fell into his hands. Four of them he burnt, and three he let go. Two were fitted up to serve as tenders. Thus strengthened, our "gentlemen of fortune" paid a visit to India, and were returning from that rich country when they met three large ships near the island of Madagascar. Two of these barely, deserting their consort, escaped. The other, commanded by one Captain Mackra, was taken after a desperate resistance; and Mackra's life was preserved with much difficulty. Through the clemency of Captain England, Mackra was allowed to depart in a badly shattered sloop, in which, I believe, he at length reached Bombay. But this clemency soon led to England's deposition. A rumor was circulated ere long that Mackra was fitting out a force against them. Upon this pretext the pirate crew marooned England upon the island of Mauritius, and left him to perish; but he, escaping to Madagascar, spent the rest of his days among the pirate colony there.

EDWARD ENGLAND'S FLAG

EDWARD ENGLAND

"Marooned"

John Evans

JOHN EVANS.

Careening.

JOHN EVANS was a Welshman born, but early in life drifted over to West Indies. Falling out of employment, he took a canoe and three or four companions, and in the month of September, 1722, started out from Port Royal harbor to seek his fortune. The first night these bold rovers went ashore, broke open several houses, and secured a considerable sum of money, with which they returned to their boat. This was all very well in its way; but Captain Evans was impatient to get to sea, and conduct business on a grander scale. In a few days he found a vessel which he thought suitable to his purpose; he went aboard, informed the crew that he was

captain of the craft, and so sailed away. Off Martinique he captured a rich prize, shared the plunder amongst his piratic crew, and retired to a secluded retreat to enjoy his honest gains. At length pinching poverty again he urged the pirates forth upon new adventures. The "Lucretia and Catherine," Captain Mills commander, was the first to fall in their way. They made the crew prisoners, manned her with pirates, and steered for Avis to careen. On the way Evans had some words with his boatswain, who was a surly, disorderly fellow. A challenge to a duel was the result, but when the ship reached land, the cowardly boatswain refused to fight, whereupon the bold Captain Evans began to drub him soundly with his cane. But, before anyone could prevent it, the boatswain slipped out a pistol, and pulling the trigger, sent a bullet crashing through the captain's head. The murderer was seized, lashed to the mast and shot. The piratic crew then disbanded, and were heard of no more.

Captain William Fly

WILLIAM FLY

Lashing a prisoner.

CAPTAIN FLY was a ranting pirate of the "Blackbeard" stripe. His low birth, and meager education barely fitted him for the villainous business he was in, but what he lacked on this score, he more than supplied by his proficiency in cruelty, profanity, and other like accomplishments. In April 1726, Fly shipped from Jamaica as boatswain to Captain Green of the sloop, Elizabeth. For a fortnight all went happily enough. Then Fly began to lay his devilish schemes. A number of the men, like himself, were ripe for any villainy. They plotted to seize the ship, murder the captain and mate, and run off pirating. This interesting programme was faithfully performed. At a given signal, Capt. Green was seized; dragged on deck, and, though begging piteously for life, was thrown overboard. The same cruel fate awaited the mate; there was no eye to pity. A quick scuffle, a dull splash, and all was over. The ship was turned about and headed for North Carolina. No pirate that ever sailed under a black flag was more ambitious of power than Fly. The commerce of all those seas was apparently within his grasp, and he intended to grasp it. He cruised up the coast, taking a number of prizes, and frightening woefully the good people along shore. Sometimes when in a passion, he would order a prisoner to the gears, and there flog him unmercifully. But swift punishment soon overtook him. He had reached the latitude of Nantucket. The prisoners, seizing their opportunity, turned on their captors, flung them under hatches, and hurried into port. A few days later William Fly swung from a Boston gibbet.

PIERRE FRANÇOIS

Capture of the Vice-Admiral. PIERRE-FRANÇOIS.

THE DARING DEEDS of a certain pirate by the name of Pierre François soon gained for him a great reputation among the lawless adventurers of Tortuga. His little brigantine, manned by a crew of six-and-twenty desperadoes, was accustomed to waylay the rich merchant ships bound from Maracaybo to Campeche. He had been now a long time at sea. Provisions were running low, his boat was leaky, the crew, moody and half mutinous. At length a pirate, more bold than the rest, suggested a visit to the South American pearl fisheries. The hazard was great, 'tis true, but, if successful, they would be enriched for life. The course was immediately changed, and away they flew to the southward.

They found the pearl fleet riding at anchor off the coast of Venezuela. Pierre hovered in the distance, and reconnoitered the situation. Rather than to return to Tortuga unsuccessful, he resolved to swoop down upon the store ship, and carry her off in the sight of all the rest of the fleet. So running boldly into the midst of the fleet, he suddenly attacked the vice-admiral under the very guns of the man-of-war convoy, took his ship, and would have gotten her safely away, together with her store of more than 100,000 pieces of eight, had he not, in his flight, overloaded her with sail, so that the mainmast went by the board. The wrathful man-of-war, in hot pursuit, overtook him; and the prize was lost. But even in this extremity Pierre's courage did not desert him; and he made so brave a stand that the Spaniards were glad enough to make terms with him for the surrender of the ship, whereby Pierre and all his crew came off scot-free.

John Gow

JOHN GOW.

THE LITTLE THAT IS KNOWN of the brief career of John Gow furnishes a story of unexcelled brutality, wickedness and crime. It was in the year 1724 that an Amsterdam galley sailed out of port on a voyage to Barbary. Among the crew was one John Gow, an evil spirit, who found a number of his own ilk on board. Among these he plotted; and, at a preconcerted signal, a band of conspirators seized the inoffensive captain, severed his throat from ear to ear, and tried to throw him overboard. The captain resisted with all his strength, whereupon the infuriated Gow flashed out his pistol, and with a dreadful oath, shot him dead. The chief mate and the clerk begged for a moment to pray, but

their entreaties were spurned, and they were likewise cruelly murdered. Then one of the red handed men came on deck, and striking a gun with his cutlass, cried, "You are welcome, Captain Gow, to your new command." Gow in reply, promised that any who disobeyed orders should go the same way the captain had gone. This said, he ordered the course to be changed to the northward. Several vessels fell into their hands, but none of them contained any considerable plunder. At length the pirates reached the Orkney Islands, where they intended to clean, but being driven ashore, were all apprehended and brought to London. At the trial Gow obstinately refused to plead; he was suspended by the thumbs till they broke, and then was ordered to be pressed to death. When the preparations were completed his courage failed him, he sullenly pleaded not guilty. The jury, however, brought in a different verdict, and Gow soon after suffered the pirate's death at Execution Dock.

SIEUR DE GRAMMONT

SIEUR DE GRAMMONT was a French gentleman, born in Paris. His gadding disposition and robust young manhood naturally drifted him towards the El Dorado of the century - the Spanish West Indies. Here he joined the freebooters; and since he was in such infamous company, he resolved to be chief among them. But his early enterprises were singularly unfortunate and discouraging for a freebooter. It was not until he linked his fortunes with that notorious pirate, Van Horn, that he gained any considerable booty. He returned from the pillage of Vera Cruz with a round fortune in good Spanish doubloons; but a single year of wild dissipation sufficed to squander all the treasure he had gained. Grammont was again utterly impoverished. Another expedition was determined upon. Twelve hundred desperadoes rushed to his standards. The piratic squadron set sail for Campeche in the month of June, 1685. The city fell. The garrison, seeing resistance hopeless, abandoned the fort, and the

pirates exultingly took possession. They found in the fort only two young officers who refused to disgracefully abandon their posts. Grammont was touched by their bravery, and ordered their property to be respected. After seven weeks' stay at Campeche, Grammont returned with his fleet to St. Domingo, soon afterwards to be honored by the appointment of King's lieutenant. But, previous to the arrival of his commission, he requested that he might make one more cruise. He therefore hastily embarked. The object of the expedition was not known. Grammont, his ship, and all his men disappeared, and were never heard of afterwards.

SIEUR DE GRAMMONT.

Entering the Fort

LAURENCE DE GRAFF

LAURENCE DE GRAFF was one of three daring buccaneer chieftains who in 1683 united under the leadership of the truculent Van Horn upon a celebrated expedition against the rich and populous city of Vera Cruz. For many years previous he was engaged in the service of Spain. He had even cruised against the freebooters, but at length fell into their hands, and himself joined the brotherhood. Knowing that if he was ever taken by the Spaniards he would certainly be beheaded, De Graff never fought without having a gunner with a lighted match ready to blow up the powder magazine at the first signal. The expedition to Vera Cruz consisted of an army of twelve hundred veteran pirates, armed to the teeth. Like a legion of demons they descended upon the unhappy city. Poverty and ruin followed in their train. In a very short time these demoniac men collected $6,000,000 in plunder. In addition they extorted another million of dollars as a ransom for the town. Then they set sail carrying with them fifteen hundred hostages. Most of these unfortunates afterwards died of sheer starvation. On the voyage Laurence and Van Horn fell into a right royal dispute. A duel was determined upon, and in the contest of arms Van Horn lost his life. Laurence returned to St. Domingo with a large share of the plunder. He afterwards conducted many piratical expeditions against the English at Jamaica as well as against the Spaniards. Of his end we know nothing, but it is supposed that he lived to a good old age.

DE GRAFF.

Duel with Van Horn.

John Halsey

CAPTAIN HALSEY

The Dutchman acquainted them of their error.

A LARGE MAJORITY of the West India and Madagascar pirates hailed from good Old England; but Captain John Halsey was born in Boston town, and passed his childhood days in that center of intellectual life and culture. Later he became captain of a privateer; and, while cruising off Cape Verde, he was impressed with the advantages offered by the corsair's life. But Captain Halsey, late of Boston, would be no ordinary, vulgar pirate; he would select his prey with consideration. Accordingly he contented himself with the rich commerce of the Moors, and so maintained very good terms with the stronger European nations. His first encounter was with a great ship of

BRONZE
NESTING WEIGHTS

sixty guns which he met in the Red Sea. Halsey at once recognized her as of Dutch build, and proceeded on his way, but the crew insisted that she was a Moor, placed a man at the helm, and was preparing to clap her on board, when a well-aimed shot from the Dutchman acquainted them of their error. The pirates ran for their lives, and at length escaped. Soon afterwards they overtook a Bengal ship. But as yet they had gained no money. For many months, their luck was steadily against them. Then they encountered and took two large ships, richly laden. One of these prizes they dismissed; and with the other they proceeded joyfully to Madagascar. That night when Captain Halsey, seated in the great cabin, reckoned up his accounts, he chuckled as he set down the round sum of fifty thousand pounds as the profit of the day's business. In due time the pirates arrived at Madagascar; and it was here that Captain Halsey was stricken down with a fever and died.

WALTER KENNEDY

WALTER KENNEDY was educated as a London thief, afterwards drifted into a piratic career, and served as lieutenant to Captain Bartholomew Roberts, the pirate. While on the coast of Guiana, he ran off with Roberts' largest cruiser, the "Rover," together with a rich Portuguese prize, recently captured, and directed his course to Barbadoes. Here he captured a vessel from Virginia, commanded by a certain Captain Knot, a Quaker. His equanimity amid misfortune so much attracted the pirates that eight of them joined him, and the honest captain took them safe to Virginia, where they were promptly arrested and hanged. Off Jamaica, Kennedy captured a flour vessel; a number of the men, who were anxious to settle down and quietly enjoy their gains, embarked in this ship. Kennedy had gone on board unobserved. His own men feared his treachery; and, when he was discovered, they would have thrown him overboard, but the rogue took the most solemn oaths of fidelity, and at

length was suffered to proceed. Kennedy knew little about navigation and his men knew less; they directed their course as best they could toward Ireland, but instead, they ran ashore on the coast of Scotland. The pirates dispersed. Most of them, betrayed by their riotous behaviour, were arrested and executed. Their infamous captain soon squandered his money, and then became a highway robber. Finally he was apprehended, and, upon the testimony of the mate of a ship he had plundered, was convicted. A few months later, this accomplished pirate, thief, and highwayman paid the legitimate penalty of his crimes at Execution Dock.

WALTER KENNEDY'S FLAG

Captain Lewis

CAPTAIN LEWIS.

Chasing a merchantman.

CAPTAIN LEWIS was an early pirate; and, during the short span of his life, attained considerable distinction in his worthy profession. He was not more than fifteen years of age when he was captured on board the pirate "Banister," and brought into Jamaica hanging by the middle from the mizzen-peak of an English man-of-war. After that he began business on his own account. He captured many small coasters and, at length, secured a large pink. In this he cruised about in the Bay of Campeche. Presently a fleet of merchantmen put out to sea. Honest Captain Lewis hugged the shore, and waited. Suddenly, like a

SUNDIAL COMPASS

hawk on its prey, he darted in among them, fired a few balls across the bows of the leading ships, and brought the whole fleet to. One by one the ships were visited and plundered. The largest sloop he fitted up for his own use, and then made his way to the Gulf of Florida. With his little squadron, he swept the entire coast as far up as Newfoundland, taking many rich ships on the way. It was the custom of these pirates, after they had skimmed the cream from American water, to hide away to Africa, and there fill out their princely fortunes from the rich commerce of the Royal African Company. Captain Lewis, no less insatiate in his lust for plunder, left Newfoundland, and steered for the coast of Guinea. Here he remained for some time, and took a great many merchant ships. At length the desperadoes who composed his crew quarreled among themselves; and, in the dispute which followed, Lewis was killed, and his quarter-master succeeded to the command.

Francis Lolonois

FRANCIS LOLONOIS.

Death of Lolonois.

FRANCIS LOLONOIS, a Frenchman, was one of the most villainous of those pirates who ravaged sea and land, calling themselves buccaneers, and assuming that they were conducting a sort of legitimate warfare in robbing the Spaniards. Cruising off Maracaybo, he captured a rich prize laden with plate, and here he conceived the plan of descending upon the city itself. So he collected seven hundred picking scoundrels from Tortuga, and taking with him, Michael le Basque, as land captain, and a certain Pierre le Picard as pilot, he swept down upon the doomed city. There was no resisting this mighty avalanche. The inhabitants

fled the town. The pirates marched in. Then began a holocaust of passion, of torture, and of blood. Gibraltar, forty leagues southward, suffered a like fate. Four awful weeks the pirates remained at Gibraltar, reveling and pillaging; and when, at length, they spread their sails, they carried with them from the tortured towns, more than $500,000 in plunder. But Lolonois's star was now destined to decline. His next expedition proved to be his last. While taking on water along the coast of Darien, his whole band was captured by one of the fiercest tribes of Indians in all that region. Most of the pirates were burned alive, but a less merciful death was reserved for Lolonois. He was bound to a tree. Hour after hour, according to their custom, the savages tortured him. At length, weary with this demoniac pastime, they hewed off his limbs, one after the other, and cast them into the flames, and his whole body was consumed to ashes. Such was the miserable life, and such the miserable death of Francis Lolonois.

Captain Edward Low

EDWARD LOW.

Torturing a Yankee.

AMONG ALL THE BLOOD-THIRSTY pirates of the seventeenth and eighteenth centuries, there was none who mounted to loftier altitudes of unprovoked and unscrupulous wickedness than Captain Edward Low. It was under a Yankee captain that he made his first voyage down to Honduras, to steal logwood from the Spaniards. But he did not long remain with his employers; for, not liking the wood-chopping business, he up with a musket and blazed away at the captain by way of farewell, and then, with twelve companions, put out to sea in a whale-boat, captured a brig, and declared war against the world. Not long afterwards he met the notorious Captain Lowther, who added the finishing touches to his education, and taught him what villainy he did not already know. Many an unhappy merchantman fell into the hands of this monster, who murdered men for sport as much as for revenge. He bore an inveterate hatred to all Yankees, and it was his custom to slit the nose and cut off the ears of all he caught. One day he sailed into Marblehead and found thirteen vessels lying in the harbor. It was a glorious day for our captain, so he took what he wanted, and sailed away. Then followed a horrible succession of barbarities, until, at length, the cruel hearts of his own demonic followers were moved to sympathy, and they refused to obey his orders when commanded to disembowel some harmless passengers on board a fishing boat off Rhode Island. Of the end of this worthy we know nothing; but we do know that, long years ago, he passed away, to answer for his deeds at the bar of Him whom his wicked life denied.

EDWARD LOW'S FLAG

GEORGE LOWTHER

GEORGE LOWTHER.

Death of Lowther.

IT WAS ABOUT THE MIDDLE of the year 1721 that George Lowther, mate of the stout ship, "Gambia Castle," determined to seize the vessel, and steer for the Spanish Main. With nine-and-forty companions won over, he slipped out of the river Gambia, in Africa, re-christened his vessel the "Happy Deliver," and steered for Barbadoes. Many were the poor merchant ships that fell a prey to this sea-hawk. During his piratic career of about three years, he swept the coasts and bays from Newfoundland to Guiana. At length, after a successful cruise to the northward, he came to the West Indies, and sought out the secluded, uninhabited island of Blanco, situated not far from Tortuga. He ran into a small cove, sent his guns, sails, and rigging ashore, and put his vessel upon the careen. In the uncomfortable position he was spied by the "Eagle" sloop of Barbadoes, who at once suspected he was a pirate, and took the opportunity to attack him. The pirates fought with the utmost desperation; but all to no avail. Just as their vessel struck, Lowther and twelve of his men escaped out of the cabin window. The master of the "Eagle," with twenty-five men, immediately set out in pursuit, and succeeded in capturing a number of the pirates, but Lowther, the most obdurate of them all, still eluded their search. The "Eagle" returned with her prisoners to Cumana. Meanwhile the pirate Lowther died by his own hand, a wretched, hopeless suicide. A few days later some straggling sailors found his body stretched beside a bush, and in his hand a pistol, burst and empty.

Edward Mansvelt

MANSVELT.

Setting out on a cruise.

THE SUCCESSFUL EXPEDITION of that early buccaneer, Lewis Scott, against the town of Campeche, inspired a notorious sea-robber, by the name of Mansvelt, to similar undertakings. This buccaneer, having collected a large body of desperadoes, landed in the Kingdom of Granada, devastated the country, and returned to Jamaica laden with spoils. In the streets of Kingston, he met Henry Morgan, captain of the freebooters, afterwards Governor of Jamaica, and knighted by King Charles II. Mansvelt appointed him vice-admiral of a new expedition, which he was at that time fitting out. A fleet of fifteen vessels was presently ready for sea. Down they swooped upon the Island of Saint Catharine (now Old Providence). The little garrison of Spanish soldiers was overwhelmed, and one hundred veteran pirates marched up and took possession. It was evidently the intention of Mansvelt to convert the island into a pirates' stronghold. Accordingly he directed his men to put the island in the best posture for defense. Meanwhile he pursued his way down the coast of Costa Rica intending to pillage all the seaport towns as he returned; but the Governor of Panama, getting wind of the expedition, roused the whole country and promptly expelled the pirates. Mansvelt repaired with his fleet to Saint Catharine. Thence he sailed to Jamaica for recruits and confidently applied to the English Governor for aid. The Governor received the pirate courteously, and expressed regret that he was unable to furnish assistance. Mansvelt then hastened to Tortuga, the celebrated rendezvous of the buccaneers, and was busily enlisting recruits when death put an end to his robberies and his career.

THE ISLAND OF TORTUGA LOOKS LIKE A MONSTER SEA-TURTLE

Sieur de Montauban

SIEUR DE MONTAUBAN.

A FEW MUSTY PAGES, written by the Sieur de Montauban himself, contain all that has been chronicled of the voyages and adventures of this famous freebooter. At the age of sixteen he took to the sea, and for twenty years on the coasts of Mexico, Florida, West Indies and Guinea, waged relentless war in the name of his king — while he himself took good care of the proceeds. In September, 1604, he sailed into Bordeaux with three fine vessels in tow, which he captured off Barbadoes. Montauban felt so well pleased with himself that he thought he would like to try his luck down on the coast of Guinea. So away he sailed, picking up a few ships and encountering some lively adventures. At length, while cruising off Angola, he was spied by an English guard-ship of fifty-four guns. She bore directly down upon him, and without further ado, prepared to board, but the grappling irons failing to catch, the stern of the man-of-war fouled the freebooters bowsprit. Montauban, observing the enemy thus encumbered, poured in volley after volley in quick succession, and the English seemed about to surrender, when, suddenly, without a moment's warning, an awful shock, followed by a terrific explosion, hurled both ships high into the air. The English captain, hoping to get off in his boats, had laid a train to the powder magazine. Only fifteen of the freebooters survived. All bruised and bleeding they paddled their way to the African shore, and ultimately reached France. The hitherto undaunted Montauban was now happily cured of his adventurous humor, and safe at home, contented himself with a recital of his exploits.

FLINTLOCK PISTOL

John Martel

In the good old days of wooden bottoms and tenpounders, when pirates swarmed about the islands and keys of the West Indies like bees about a hive, there was a pirate by the name of John Martel, whose career, though brief, was filled with wild and daring adventures. Martel appeared about the year 1716 as captain of a piratic sloop cruising in Jamaica waters. He presently fell in with the good ship "Berkley," which he captured and plundered of about five thousand dollars in money. Fortune seemed to smile upon his endeavors. In rapid succession twelve more handsome prizes were captured. After being plundered they were generally turned adrift. At length the pirates concluded to go into port, and refresh themselves after their fatigues. Accordingly they repaired to the island of Santa Cruz, stowed snugly away their little squadron of five sail in the secluded harbor, and then gave themselves up to the enjoyment of the occasion. But all this felicity was destined to be rudely dissipated. The "Scarborough," a royal man-of-war, receiving information of this nest of pirates, immediately sailed down to the island and, bringing her guns to bear, silenced the piratic batteries and sunk one of the ships. For several days the man-of-war stood off and on, and blockaded the little harbor. Then the pirates, endeavoring to warp out and escape, ran aground; and, seeing the "Scarborough" bearing down upon them, they deserted their ship, consigned her to the flames, and fled to the woods. It is supposed they perished there as they were never heard of afterwards.

CAPTAIN MARTEL.

Escaping the Scarborough.

MONTBAR.

Fight with Spanish Men-of-war.

THERE WAS A CELEBRATED PIRATE born in Languedoc, name Montbar, who seems to have been inspired with a maniacal hatred against the whole Spanish nation. During the process of his education, he brooded over the almost incredible cruelties practiced upon the Indians by the Spaniards

during their conquest of America. His reason even became disturbed, and he regarded himself as marked out by God to avenge these wrongs. His first step was to enlist on board a French man-of-war which was just starting on a cruise against the Spaniards. Each time he met the enemy, he fought with the utmost recklessness. Always first to board, he mowed down all he could reach. Meanwhile he was placed in command of one of the prizes. His most desperate engagement followed shortly afterwards. Encountering two large Spanish war ships off the West Indies, he attacked them with fury, sinking one and boarding the other. Rushing up and down the decks, he put to the sword all that resisted. Montbar now had two ships at his command. He engaged many buccaneers in his service; and swept the seas, often landing and ravaging the coasts. He died, probably, unconscious of crime, unpitying and unpitied.

Peter the Great

PETER THE GREAT.

Boarding the Galleon.

THERE WAS AT TORTUGA, an island just north of St. Domingo, a man born in Dieppe, Normandy. From his gigantic stature he was familiarly called Peter the Great. According to most writers he was the first successful pirate at Tortuga. He took a boat, and with twenty-eight companions, desperate men, he set out in search of booty. They were almost in despair, when, one afternoon, to their joy, they espied in the distance a sail. As they approached it, they were somewhat alarmed to discover a huge Spanish galleon, laden to the gunwales with treasure. The crew was well armed,

and without a doubt had some heavy guns on board. Peter addressed his men in a glowing speech, arousing them to a frenzy of courage. They resolved to take the ship or die in the attempt. The wind favored the pirates. The night was dark. They ran alongside the bulk of the galleon so noiselessly that they were not perceived. Rushing pell-mell on board, they cut down the terrified crew. Peter leading a party, plunged into the cabin, where he found the captain. Presenting a pistol to his breast, he demanded the surrender of the ship. Had the officers attempted the slightest resistance, death would have been their immediate fate. They were all disarmed and bound. In a very few minutes this majestic ship, with its vast treasures, was captured. Not a single pirate was killed. Exulting in their victory, they landed the Spanish Captain and crew on an island, and turned the ship towards Europe. Upon their arrival in France they sold their ship, divided the immense treasure, and were heard of no more.

PIERRE LE PICARD

AMONG THE TRUCULENT BUCCANEERS of Tortuga, there was a remarkable man, of great resources, by the name of Pierre le Picard. He was a bold soldier and a hardy seaman. Fearless and unscrupulous, at the first notice of the great expedition of Francis Lolonois, against the powerful city of Maracaybo, Pierre enlisted, and became the pilot of the fleet. It was his skillful hand that guided the piratic squadron over the bar at the entrance of Maracaybo harbor, and no one participated more actively than he in all the cruel enormities that followed. Afterwards, Pierre accompanied Lolonois on his fatal expedition to the coast of Nicaragua. When, at length, even the vice-admiral, Moses Vauclin, foreseeing that the expedition must result in failure, deserted in his swift-sailing ship, Pierre went with him. Then this bold robber joined his fortunes with Sir Henry Morgan, and was received into his esteem by this arch-pirate. During the expedition against Caraccas, Morgan met with

many discouragements. His fleet of fifteen vessels and 900 men had dwindled to eight vessels and 500 men. It was folly to attempt his original design with forces so reduced. In this emergency, Pierre le Picard came forward with a plan, which he proposed with all the rude eloquence of sincerity. It was nothing less than a second attack upon Maracaybo. A council of officers was called, and the scheme was rapturously approved. The fleet immediately weighed anchor, and soon the doomed city was again at the mercy of the spoilers. Captain Picard was very exultant in view of the success of his expedition; and here his name is lost amidst the bloodshed and confusion of pillage.

PIERRE PICARD.

Proposing his plan.

John Phillips

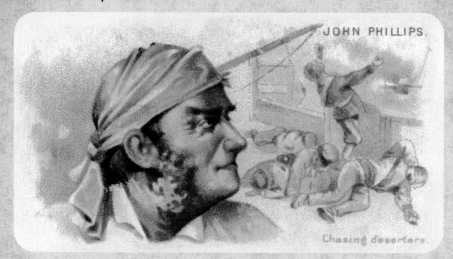

JOHN PHILLIPS.

Chasing deserters.

JOHN PHILLIPS sailed from England as carpenter of a vessel bound for Newfoundland. On the voyage Captain Anstis with his piratic squadron sighted the merchantman and ran her down. Phillips was impressed as an addition to the piratic crew. Whether willingly or not, he at length became reconciled to the life, and remained with the company until it was disbanded. Afterwards Phillips went to Newfoundland, and again set out on a piratic cruise. On the Banks several fishing vessels fell into his hands and were plundered, and many of the sailors were forced to join the pirates. Phillips then directed his course to Barbadoes. For three long months he cruised among the islands without taking a single ship. At length, he fell in with a French vessel from which he gained a large supply of provisions, of which he stood in great need. At this time there were many malcontents among the crew, so that when a few days later they captured a sloop and sent a prize crew on board to take possession, they determined to run off with her. Captain Phillips, however, soon perceived their design, and gave chase. A lively skirmish ensued, in which several of the deserters were wounded, and the others were forced to surrender. Phillips now directed his course northward to the Newfoundland coast. On the voyage they gathered in a great harvest of plunder from the many captured ships. Besides, many forced men were added to the crew. But the prisoners conspired together, rose upon the pirates, slew the captain and boatswain, threw the mate into the sea, and, having secured the rest, brought them into Boston, where they were afterwards condemned and hanged.

Raveneau de Lussan

SIR RAVENEAU DE LUSSAN.

Bargaining with the Captain.

The history of Sieur Raveneau de Lussan and his famous voyage into the South Sea, furnish one of the amplest pages in buccaneer history. Fretted by the restraints of civilized life in his native Paris, this wayward youth resolved to seek adventures in marvelous America. Accordingly, in the year 1679, he embarked for St. Domingo, where three years of toil and hardship as a planter's engage awaited him. At length, released by the interposition of the Governor, he determined to join the freebooters, and offered his services to an old filibuster named Laurence de Graff. Their fleet was soon ready to sail. For some months they cruised about in the

Caribbean; then Raveneau separated from de Graff, and joined a party of buccaneers upon an expedition across the isthmus into the South Sea. They reached the Pacific coast, not far from the city of Panama, and immediately commenced active operations against the Spaniards. The record of their exploits during the following four years would excite our admiration, did we not remember that they were spurred on to these desperate enterprises by no higher motives than an insatiate lust for gold. The flourishing Spanish towns of La Seppa, Leon, Granada, and Guayaquil fell before the invincible attack of these marauders. Finally, having endured many hardships, a party of three hundred, led by the brave and sagacious de Lussan, recrossed the isthmus to the Atlantic side, crowded, as many as could, on board a small vessel, and directed their course for St. Domingo. De Lussan later returned to France, destitute of plunder, but satisfied to behold his native land once more.

Captain Jack Rackam

Captain Jack Rackam succeeded Charles Vane as commander of a piratic brigantine. He cruised about for a time among the reefs and coral islands of the West Indies, and plundered several merchantmen. Then he took a turn among the Bermudas, where he ran down a fine ship from Carolina, and another from New England. By these acquisitions the common store was much augmented, and Rackam retired with his crew to a well-known retreat in the Island of Cuba. While he and his companions were in the midst of their wild orgies, their vessel was spied by a Spanish guard-ship which happened to be passing. In company with the Spaniard was an English prize recently taken. These two ships immediately put into the cove, and attacked the pirates. Night coming on, in order to prevent any possibility of escape, the guard-ship anchored at one entrance to the cove, while the prize anchored at the other. The pirates, roused to despair, cutlass in hand, boarded the Spanish prize at dead of night; and, threatening the crew with instant death if they made the least outcry, they captured her without losing a man. Then slipping the cable they silently stood out to sea, and disappeared beyond the horizon. But their escape was only for a time. Not many months afterwards, a swift sailing English frigate overtook them, and carried the entire piratic crew as prisoners to Jamaica, where they were tried and condemned. Captain Rackam, with four companions, was suspended at Gallows Point, Port Royal, November 17th, 1720, while the rest of his crew was sent over to Kingston to share a like fate.

JACK RACKAM'S FLAG

BARTHOLOMEW ROBERTS

THE HISTORY OF Captain Bartholomew Roberts is a tale of destruction, desolation and woe. On the 13th of January, 1722, Roberts and his piratic squadron sailed into the harbor of Whydah, on the African Coast; and, at a single blow, took eleven ships. At Martinique, he robbed twenty vessels, one after the other, and then consigned them to the flames. But at Newfoundland he made his greatest catch, and, in a single harbor, drew into the tolls a fleet of twenty-two ships. One by one they were plundered, and burned to the water's edge, while he laid waste the whole region round about. Upon one occasion, three of the pirates, weary of their wretched, sinful life, deserted, but the next day they were recaptured, and put upon trial. Sentence was about to be passed, when a member of the jury arose, and swore Glashby (one of the prisoners) should not die: 'Glashby was an honest fellow in spite of his misfortune, and he loved him, and if he must die, he would die along with him;' and, as he spoke, he handled an ugly pair of pistols and presented them at two of the judges. They, thinking the argument good, at once acquitted Glashby; but his fellow asserters were immediately tied to the mast and shot. Bart Roberts was the especial pupil of Davis, the pirate, and succeeded that worthy as captain of the fleet. The last engagement which he fought was with the "Swallow" man-of-war. He made a gallant figure, dressed in the most extravagant piratical costume, but, at the first return fire of the "Swallow," fell; and his crew, one and all, surrendered to justice and the gallows.

BARTHOLOMEW ROBERTS' FLAG

MARY READ

MARY READ.

The Duel

ABOUT TWO HUNDRED YEARS AGO, in a little town in England, Mary Read was born, and reared as a boy. After various experiences on land and sea, she shipped, disguised as a sailor boy, on board a Dutch vessel bound for the West Indies. On the voyage they were captured by pirates, and Mary Read was impressed by the pirate crew, while the despoiled merchantman and its crew were set adrift. A few months later we find Mary on board a ship under command of an old pirate named Rackham. Many richly-laden merchant ships were captured. On board one of these ships was a young English artist,

a handsome fellow, with pleasing manners, whom Rackham detained. As the two became acquainted, the whole passionate nature of the girl became aglow with love for her new friend. But a cloud came over their happiness. The young artist was grossly insulted by one of the pirates, and a duel was determined upon. Mary was in a state of the greatest anxiety for her lover. She therefore deliberately provoked the pirate to an immediate and angry challenge, and adroitly arranged for the hostile encounter to take place just two hours before the duel with the artist. She was a true shot and an admirable swordsman. The combatants met on land, and exchanged shots at close quarters. Advancing, they crossed swords, and in a moment Mary dexterously passed her weapon through the body of her antagonist, and he fell dead before her. Shortly after this event the entire pirate crew was captured, taken to Jamaica, and condemned; but Mary Read died in prison before the day of execution.

ROC BRASILIANO

ROC, THE BRAZILIAN, a name once known and feared throughout all the Spanish Main, was born in Groningen, Holland, and flourished about the same time as Barthelemy (1675). His own name being forgotten, he was dubbed "the Brazilian" on account of his long residence in Brazil. For the Spaniards, Roc always entertained an inveterate hatred, and taxed his invention for new modes of torture. It is said that he even roasted some of his prisoners alive on wooden spits like boucanned boars. On one occasion, while cruising along the coast of Campeche, his ship was wrecked by a sudden storm. Roc and his crew escaped with only their muskets, a little powder, and a few bullets. But nothing daunted, they set out at once for a famous rendezvous of pirates. After two days journey they caught sight of a well manned Spanish vessel lying off the coast. It was convoy to a company of dyewood cutters. Roc saw an opportunity to retrieve his fortunes; and, instantly concealing his band, went with six

men into ambush to watch. Early the next morning the Spaniards pulled ashore. The wily Roc at once overpowered them; and, rowing out to the ship, easily captured her. He now had a good ship under him, and his first thought was to seek for prey. He soon succeeded in capturing a rich prize, with which he repaired to Jamaica, where, in a few days, he squandered all that he had gained. Thence, urged by poverty, he put out to sea again, and for a number of years continued his career of robbery and cruelty. Without doubt, he had a miserable end, and his bones, perhaps, still whiten on some Indian Bay.

ROC THE BRAZILIAN.

Capturing boat's crew.

Captain Sawkins

SAWKINS.

Boarding Peralta's ship.

CAPTAIN SAWKINS was an English privateersman. In 1679 he joined the buccaneers, and conducted an expedition against the city of Panama. Associated with him was one Captain Sharp, whose life appears in another sketch. Sailing from their rendezvous, Sawkins and his 300 pirates landed on the eastern coast of the isthmus; and, nothing daunted by the difficulties of the way, they set out overland across the isthmus towards Panama. One month later the pirates, in 37 canoes, arrived in sight of the great city; their coming was not unknown to the Spaniards. There rode at anchor in the harbor five great ships and three

smaller armadillas. This fleet, as soon as the buccaneers hove in sight, immediately bore down upon them. Captain Sawkins, in the leading canoe, received the attack of a well-manned Spanish ship, commanded by a brave old Andalusian, Francisco de Peralto. The fight between them was desperate, each crew trying to board, and firing as quick as they could load. Suddenly a volcano of fire spouted up from the Spaniard's deck; the magazine had exploded and carried up with it half the vessel. Under cover of the smoke and confusion, Sawkins boarded and took the ship. The remaining Spanish ships, disheartened at this frightful calamity, immediately struck their colors. Sawkins now had a powerful fleet at his command. He ambitiously planned still greater undertakings, and first he steered for the Isle of Cayboa, famous for its pearl fisheries, but here his successful career was cut short, for making an attack upon a town near by, he was shot dead while running furiously up the ramparts.

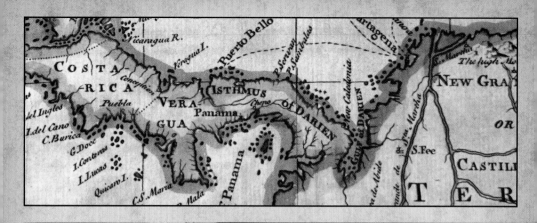

LEWIS SCOTT

LEWIS SCOT.

WHEN LEWIS SCOTT came upon the stage, "buccaneering," as it was generally called, had ceased to bring in the vast returns it once had done. The Spanish Main was infested by hundreds of reckless, ruthless pirates, insatiate in their lust for plunder and for blood. No merchantman dared venture out of port without a powerful man-of-war convoy, and even then they were not always secure from molestation. For every four vessels that once sailed not more than one could now be seen. It was evident that there must be a new departure or buccaneering would cease to exist. In this extremity Lewis Scott arose, and showed the buccaneers a new way to squeeze money from the Spaniards. As there were no longer prizes to be gained upon the sea, he determined to gain them upon land. Gathering together at Torutuga a band of desperadoes, ready for any deeds of violence and crime, he landed upon the peninsula of Yucatan, and captured and sacked the city of Campeche. When he had stripped it of everything but the tiles and the paving stones, he demanded an excessive ransom and threatened to lay the whole town in ashes unless it was promptly paid. Then having gathered together his booty he set sail and arrived safely at Tortuga.

BARTHOLOMEW SHARP

BARTHOLOMEW SHARP was an associate with Captain Sawkins upon a buccaneering expedition into the South Sea in the year 1680. Having captured the Spanish fleet that guarded the harbor of Panama, these bold buccaneers planned to cruise along the coasts of Peru and Chili, sack the wealthy seaport towns, and then, laden with Spanish doubloons and royal plate, to direct their course to Jamaica, by way of the Straits of Magellan. After the death of Sawkins, Sharp assumed the chief command; and first he led his troupe of pirates against the little town of Hilo. Next he attacked the city of La Serena, on the Peruvian coast. A hundred thousand pieces of eight were demanded as a ransom for the town. The people hesitated; but there was no hesitation on the part of Sharp. He promptly ordered the fair city to be in laid ashes. Every single house was separately fired, so as to render the destruction complete. Then Sharp and his band of robbers sailed away. For nearly two years more they continued their depredations, then finding the entire coast alarmed, and seeing no further prospect of squeezing more money from the Spaniards, Captain Sharp steered for the Straits of Magellan, and on the 28th of January, 1682, arrived at Barbadoes. Those of the company who had not already squandered their share of the plunder, won at such a cost, took passage for England. Upon their arrival, Sharp was tried for piracy, but escaping the penalty of justice, he set sail from London, with sixteen desperadoes, equally fearless as himself, and disappeared to die, no one knows where.

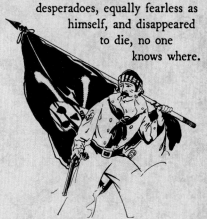

SHARP.

Firing La Serena.

83

Captain Thomas Tew

CAPTAIN TEW.

A calm, rich Christian

A CERTAIN GOVERNOR of Bermuda, the possessor of large territory but small revenues, bethought himself how he might better his fortunes. Accordingly he fitted out two privateers, commanded by Captain Thomas Tew and Captain George Drew, and instructed them to proceed to the river Gambia, in Africa, and capture the French factory of Goorie. The two commanders took their departure. For some time they kept company; then a violent storm arose, and they were separated. Captain Tew accepted his lot quite resignedly. Calling all hands on deck, he stated that their former undertaking must now result in failure, and proposed to shape a course for them which would certainly enrich them all for life. This speech, so fair and promising, quite captivated the men; and away they sailed for the straits of Babel Mandeb, as jolly a crew of pirates as ever swept the main. In the Red Sea they came up with a tall ship of India. Tew told his men that she carried their fortunes; and forthwith they ran alongside, swarmed over the gunwales, and drove the defenders below hatches. Each pirate received, as his share, more than $15,000 in plunder. Tew was now quite willing to return to America, retire from the business, and spend the rest of his life, a calm, rich Christian. He located in Rhode Island; and the good people little knew that the quiet sea captain, who lived among them, was the celebrated pirate, Captain Tew. After many years; some of his men, who lived near by, prevailed upon him to undertake one more voyage to the Red Sea. Tew yielded, and in the first engagement was struck by a cannon ball and expired.

THOMAS TEW'S FLAG

Capt. Francis Spriggs

CAPTAIN FRANCIS SPRIGGS was quarter-master to Low, and shared in all the barbarities of his execrable gang until he parted from them. In 1723, Low captured, on the Guinea coast, a stout ship, called the "Delight," and placed Spriggs in command. This bold desperado soon found an opportunity to desert, so he changed his course in the night, and left Low to vent his wrath in harmless oaths and execrations. The deserter hoisted the "Jolly Roger," made terrible with skull and cross-bones, fired all their guns, and steered for the West Indies. They first overtook a Portuguese bark, which they plundered and burnt. The crew was turned adrift. George II's birthday they spent in roaring out healths and drinking, expecting that there would be a general pardon on his accession, and vowing, if they were excepted, to murder every Englishman they met. One night, shortly afterwards, they gave chase to a merchantman, which they took to be a Spaniard. Coming up close upon her, they poured in two deadly broadsides. Then a lamentable cry for quarter went up from the ship; and the pirates discovered that it was a logwood vessel which they had turned adrift three days before, shattered, and battered, and worthless. They rushed upon the harmless captain, dragged him into the cabin, and, as a punishment, forced him to eat a dish of candles. His ship, meanwhile, did service as a huge bonfire to illuminate their midnight orgies. After perpetrating many other nameless horrors, Spriggs was, at length, driven from West Indian waters by a French man-of-war. He directed his course towards Newfoundland, disappeared, never to be heard of afterwards.

FRANCIS SPRIGGS.

Prisoner eating candles

Captain Charles Vane

CHARLES VANE.

Defying the Governor.

Captain Charles Vane began his piratic career by stealing silver from the Spaniards; and taking a liking to the business, he extended his operations so as to include other nations as well. When Governor Rogers arrived with his English fleet at the island of Providence in the year 1718, Charles Vane was one of the piratic chieftains whom he found at this famous colony of rogues. All the other pirates submitted, but not so Charles Vane. On the other hand he immediately slipped his cable, and, defiantly flaunting his piratic colors, sailed out of the harbor. Vane cruised about the Bahamas for a time. Then he up and blockaded the port of

Charleston, and afterwards sent the brave Colonel Rhet (the same who afterwards captured Stede Bonnet, the pirate) on a wild-goose chase to the southward, while he sailed up the coast, and paid a visit to the famous Blackbeard. Not long afterwards Captain Vane was deposed; and Jack Rackam, the quarter-master, succeeded to the command. Vane and a few adherents were placed aboard a sloop, supplied with a little ammunition, and left to shift for themselves. They directed their course for West Indian waters, and in the Bay of Honduras captured the "Pearl," from Jamaica. Vane was soon wrecked, however, upon a small island, and was supported by fishermen. At length a ship, which put into the island, took him on board. It now seemed probable that this notorious pirate would escape the penalty which his crimes merited. But by chance he was recognized by the captain of a passing vessel. He was immediately put in irons, and upon arrival at Jamaica was duly tried and executed.

Van Horn

VAN HORN.

Striking down a coward.

THERE WAS A CELEBRATED PIRATE by the name of Van Horn, whose daring deeds, truculent cruelty, and large fortune, had raised him to great prominence among the society of freebooters. He was originally a common Dutch sailor, and had made his money a-pirating in European waters. Finally he decided to pay a visit to the Spanish Main. Upon his arrival at Porto Rico, he boldly entered the harbor; and, finding a fleet of Spanish galleons about to sail for Europe, he gallantly offered to act as convoy. The Spaniards were inconsiderate enough to accept. The fleet put out to sea. They were soon out of sight of land. Then the crafty Dutchman suddenly seized two of the ships that were most richly laden, and made off with them. This bold stroke put him in possession of immense wealth. He now lavished the most magnificent rewards upon his companions, as he had, with his own hand, struck down any who, during the battle, had betrayed the slightest symptoms of fear. Such was Van Horn when he joined the freebooters upon an expedition more adventurous than any he had yet undertaken. This was nothing less than the sacking of the powerful city of Vera Cruz. The town was promptly surprised, ransacked, and more than $7,000,000 in plunder carried off. The return of the pirates, however, was marked by a fatal accident. Van Horn quarreled with one of his vice-admirals, named De Graff. Their dispute rose to such a height that they came to a duel, in which Van Horn was mortally wounded. The ships of the fleet were dispersed, and part fell into the hands of the Spaniards; a part, tossed by tropical tempests, were never heard of more.

"Dutch Onion" refering to its shape, from the early 1700's. It was a utility bottle for rum, wine, vinegar or oils.

MOSES VAUCLÍN

MOSES VAUCLIN was one of those wild spirits who accompanied that most atrocious of pirates, Francis Lolonois, on his last and fatal expedition to the coast of Nicaragua. Vauclin served as lieutenant. The fleet set sail in the year 1667. They touched the continent on the inhospitable shores of Honduras, five hundred miles west of the point they wished to make. Successive forages could scarcely supply enough food each day to feed seven hundred hungry mouths. At length they learned that in the river Montagua, about 60 miles west of their present station, there was a large ship recently arrived from Spain. Four boats crowded with pirates were immediately dispatched to capture the ship. Moses Vauclin led the attacking party. The ship was gallantly defended, but the veteran pirates soon became masters. Lieutenant Vauclin was placed in charge of the splendid ship. She was a swift sailer and well equipped. About this time loud murmurs of discontent arose. Vauclin determined to desert. Having gained over his crew of one hundred and fifty men, he silently raised anchor in the dead of night, spread the sail, and before the morning light, disappeared beyond the horizon. The fugitives could not think of returning penniless to Tortuga. They coasted southward as far as Costa Rica. Here they landed and boldly attacked the Spanish town of Veraguas, but obtained little booty. The Spaniards rallied in great numbers. The pirates, alarmed, hastened to their ship, and returned to Tortuga. Vauclin afterwards accompanied other piratical expeditions, and, at length, through crime and misery, found his way to death and the judgment seat.

MOSES VAUCLIN.

Captain Worley

CAPTAIN WORLEY.

Setting out from New York

CAPTAIN WORLEY was a townsman of Captain Kidd; and about sixteen years after that worthy shuffled off so tragically at Execution Dock, this bold adventurer started out to make himself rich and famous, and with no intention of coming to the same disastrous end. With eight companions he set out from New York Harbor in the month of September, 1718, in a small open boat. Upon reaching the Delaware River, they turned up, and, in the vicinity of New Castle, captured a shallop laden with household goods and plate. They relieved the poor terrified captain of all the valuable part of his cargo and then let him go. A few days afterwards an English sloop, well armed and well provisioned, fell into their hands. The pirates tumbled on board, drove the crew below hatches, and stood boldly out to sea. After a six weeks' cruise they appeared off the coast of South Carolina. Worley had by this time increased his crew to twenty-five men. With characteristic boldness he planned an extensive cruise upon the Carolinian coast, famous as the scene of Blackbeard's piracies, but the brave Colonel Johnson, the then governor of the province, suddenly put an end both to his life and to his schemes. Having dispatched four swift sailing sloops to engage this pirate, he was discovered just outside of Charleston bar. There was a hot exchange of broadsides for a time, and then down came the "black Roger." The loss on board the piratic ship was very great. Worley himself was among the first to fall, and lay dead upon the deck. The survivors were carried into Charleston amid great public rejoicing, and the following day were duly executed at White Point.

CAPTAIN WORLEY'S FLAG

AFT: The back part of a ship.

ANCHOR: A heavy weight on a chain or rope that is lowered to the seafloor to hold a ship in one location.

ASTROLABE: A navigation device used by sailors for thousands of years to find their approximate location at sea. Used to measure the angle between the horizon and the sun or a specific star, to determine the ship's latitude.

BALLAST: Stones, bricks or heavy cargo placed in the bottom of a ship to help make it more stable.

BAR: A sandbank often found just beneath the waves at the entrance to an inlet or harbor where it creates a hazard to ships. Bars can often only be crossed at high tide.

BARNACLE: A small shellfish that collects by the thousands on the underwater part of a ship's hull. They greatly reduce the speed of the ship.

BEAM: The width of a ship's hull.

BECALMED: A sailing ship that cannot move because there is no wind.

BILGE: The lowest area of a ship where all the dirty water and liquids from the upper decks collects.

BINNACLE: Usually located next to the ship's wheel, it provides a protective covering for the ship's compass.

BLACK JACK: A mug made of leather coated in tar that was popular for serving wine and beer in taverns.

BLOCK AND TACKLE: Pulleys and ropes arranged to make it easier for sailors to lift heavy loads or to raise sails.

BOARD: To get on a ship. Armed men sent to capture a ship were members of a "boarding party."

BOATSWAIN OR BOSUN: Ship's officer responsible for sails, anchors, rigging and the gear used to operate them.

BOW: The front of a ship's hull.

BOWSPRIT: A long wooden pole that extends from the front (bow) of a ship.

BROADSIDE: The firing of all the guns on one side of ship at the same time.

BUCCANEER: A general term applied to pirates operating in the West Indies and along the coast of Central and South America.

BULKHEAD: A vertical "wall" that separates compartments in a ship.

BUMBOE: An alcoholic drink made from sugar cane flavored with spices.

CAPSTAN: A large, vertical winch that could be turned by the ship's crew to raise the anchor or pull heavy cables.

CAREEN: A maintenance technique that leans a ship over so far that the crew can scrape barnacles and other growth from the underside of the hull.

CARGO: The goods being transported aboard a ship.

CAROUSING: To go on drinking binges that sometimes lasted for several days.

CARTOGRAPHER: A map maker.

CAT-O-NINE-TAILS: A whip made of nine strands with knots used to painfully punish sailors.

CAULK: To stop a ship's hull from leaking by plugging holes or gaps with fiber and tar.

CHAIN-SHOT: Two cannon balls linked with a chain and fired from a single gun to tear apart sails and rigging.

CHART: A nautical map used in sailing that shows important coastal and sea features.

COLORS: The flags flown on a ship to show its nationality.

COMPASS: A navigation instrument with a magnetized needle that always points north.

CODE OF CONDUCT: A standard list of rules for pirate behavior.

CORSAIR: A French word for pirate often applied to pirates in the Mediterranean Sea.

CROW'S NEST: Lookout post on a platform atop the main mast of a ship.

CUTLASS: A short sword with a wide flat blade popular among pirates because it did not get caught in the rigging as would a longer sword blade.

DEADEYE: A round wooden block with three holes that is used in adjusting the tension of the rigging.

DEAD RECKONING: Estimating a ship's position and speed by observing wind, waves, currents, birds and other factors known only to experienced sailors.

DOUBLOON: English word for a gold Spanish coin worth 16 pieces of eight. Spanish word for this coin is escudo.

DRAFT: The depth of water needed to float a particular ship or boat.

FATHOM: A measurement of water depth equal to six feet.

FILIBUSTER: French term for pirate.

FLAGSHIP: A fleet commander's ship.

FLIP: A drink made from beer and sugar cane alcohol. Usually heated and served in a tin cup.

FLOGGING: Punishing a sailor by striking him with a whip on his bare back. The number of lashes he received was determined by the seriousness of his crime.

FORE: The forward part of a ship.

FREEBOOTER: Dutch term for a pirate.

FURL: To lower a sail, wrap it tightly around a spar and tie it in place.

GROG: A drink made of one part rum and two parts water.

GUNWALE: The highest level of wooden planking covering the sides of a ship.

HARDTACK: A hard, dried biscuit that was frequently eaten at sea.

HELM: The wheel or tiller that is used to steer a ship.

HELMSMAN: The sailor who uses the helm to steer the ship.

HOGSHEAD: A large wooden barrel or cask used to transport both dry and liquid goods.

HOLD: A large open area below the main deck where cargo is stored.

HULL: The structure that forms the body or shell of a ship. It floats on the water and the masts and other parts of the ship are attached to it.

JOLLY ROGER: A pirate flag featuring a white skull and crossed bones.

KEELHAULED: A punishment in which a person is tied to a rope, thrown overboard and pulled through the water, passing beneath the ship.

KNOT: A measurement of a ship's speed through the water in nautical miles per hour. A nautical mile is 796 feet longer than a land mile.

LANDLUBBER: Anyone not a sailor.

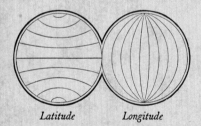

Latitude   *Longitude*

LATITUDE: Navigation lines on a chart that horizontally encircle the Earth. Used to determine a position by distance north or south of the equator.

LEAD WEIGHT: A weight attached to the end of a line and tossed overboard to determine water depth.

LEAGUE: Distance equal to 3 miles.

LEE: The direction or position away from the wind, downwind.

LEE SHORE: The shoreline being struck directly by the wind. The shore onto which a sailing ship could be driven by the wind.

LEEWARD: The direction toward which the wind is blowing.

LETTER OF MARQUE: A written document that proves a pirate or privateer is sailing under the authority of a specified king or government.

LINE: A rope that is part of the rigging of a sailing ship.

LIST: The condition when a ship leans to one side, often as a result of a leak.

LOGBOOK: A book in which the details of a ship's voyage are recorded.

LONGITUDE: Navigation lines on a chart that vertically encircle the Earth. Used to determine a position in terms of distance east or west of the prime meridian.

MAGAZINE: The part of a ship where gunpowder and ammunition are stored.

MAROON: To intentionally abandon someone on a deserted island.

MAST: A tall, round piece of timber that supports the sails.

MIZZENMAST: Mast nearest the stern.

MOUNTED GUNS: Cannons on carriages.

MUSKET: A long, single-shot weapon that was the predecessor to the rifle.

MUTINY: A revolt by the crew against a captain and officers with the purpose of taking control of the ship

PIECES OF EIGHT: Spanish silver coin that could be divided into eight pieces.

PIRATE: A term applied to anyone who performs robbery at sea.

POOP DECK: Partial deck raised above the quarterdeck at the rear of a ship.

PORT: Facing foreward, it is the left side of a ship.

PRESIDIO: A fortified Spanish city with a permanent military garrison.

PRESS GANG: A gang that kidnapped men and forced them to join the crew.

PRIVATEER: A private vessel, its captain and crew who received official permission from a government to capture merchant vessels from an enemy country.

PRIZE: A captured ship.

QUARTERDECK: A deck above the main deck that usually extended from the stern. Ship's officers oversaw the operation of the ship from there.

RAIL: A wooden plank running along the top of the gunwale down both sides of a ship.

RATLINES: Part of the rigging used as a ladder for the sailors to reach the sails.

RIGGING: The collection of ropes that hold up the masts, secure the sails and control their movement.

RUDDER: A device protruding from the back end of a ship used for steering. It is connected to the ship's helm.

SACK: To attack, capture, plunder and often burn a city.

SAIL: Large section of cloth designed to catch the wind and move a ship through the water.

SAND GLASS: Hourglass to measure time based on how long it takes for the sand to empty from the top container to the bottom. On ships, they usually came in four sizes — 30 seconds; 30 minutes; one hour and four hours.

SCURVY: Vitamin C deficiency caused by a lack of fresh fruits and vegetables. Leading cause of death among sailors. British sailors tried to prevent it by eating limes, thus the term "limeys." Spanish sailors used oranges.

SCHOONER: A sailing ship with two masts with sails rigged in front and behind each mast.

SHIP: A sailing vessel with three or more square-rigged masts.

SHIPSHAPE: Condition of a ship that is well organized and efficiently operated.

SHROUDS: Groups of ropes that form the rigging to support the masts.

SLIP ANCHOR: To release the anchor and leave it behind on the seafloor in order to make a fast getaway.

SLOOP: A sailing vessel with a single mast rigged with a mainsail and a foresail. In the 1700s, ships with 4 to 12 guns mounted on the upper deck were known as "sloops" even when they had more than one mast.

SPAR: A round piece of timber used as a top mast, yard or to support rigging.

SQUARE-RIGGED: Sails that are at right angles to the ship's hull.

STARBOARD: Facing the front, the right hand side of the ship.

STERN: The rear of a ship's hull.

STRIKE THE COLORS: Hauling down the flag as a signal of surrender.

SWINGING THE LEAD: Tossing and retrieving a weighted line with knots marking fathoms to determine the depth of the water beneath a ship.

SWIVEL GUN: Small cannon attached to a swivel mounted on ship's gunwale.

TACK: To change the direction of a ship by turning into the wind until it blows against the sails from other side.

VICTUALS OR VITTLES: Food

WAGGONER: An atlas or collection of charts. (Named after Dutch sailor Lucas Waghenaer who published a comprehensive volume of charts and sailing information in 1584.)

WEIGH: To lift or raise something as in "weigh anchor."

WINDLASS: A winch type device used for pulling up the anchor or other heavy objects. Smaller and less powerful than a capstan, it was used aboard small vessels including fishing boats.

WINDWARD: The direction from which the wind is blowing.

YARD: A large wooden pole horizontal to the mast from which sails are set.

YARDARM: The outer end of a yard.